I N...

with gratitude,

Linda

FreeMo
JOURNALS

In response to many requests for small group and Sunday school materials, Light and Life Publishing is pleased to present the FreeMo Journals. These books have been ideally prepared for any leader to facilitate discipleship in a small group setting, or for individual Christians to employ as a resource for their daily devotions.

The FreeMo Journals cover a wide variety of topics, but have been framed around the Free Methodist Church's Nine Strategies for whole church growth.

- Rev. Jay Cordova, Publisher, Free Methodist Church - USA

If you would like to purchase more issues of the FreeMo Journals please go to:
freemethodistbooks.com

Design by Jake Blythe

CONTENTS

INTRODUCTION   1
// GERALD COATES

PIONEER MISSIONARIES
// DAVID ROLLER

    1. Going To Sea   7
    2. The Finances   17
    3. Need Not Apply?   27
    4. Past, Present, You   37

PARTNERING WITH THE INTERNATIONAL CHURCH
// LINDA ADAMS

    5. God's End Game   49
    6. Silver and Gold Might Be Nice   57
    7. The Bullseye on God's Target   67
    8. Sustaining Songs for the Overstuffed   75

REACHING CROSS CULTURALLY IN THE UNITED STATES
// GERALD COATES

    9. Start Simply: Making Friends with First Generation Immigrants   85
    10. Extend Naturally: Engaging the People We Encounter   93
    11. Increase Internally: Going Beyond the Expected   101
    12. Expand Spontaneously: Following the Lead of the Spirit   109
    13. Broaden Biblically: Understanding Hospitality   117

CONCLUSION   125
// GERALD COATES

INTRODUCTION

The destination of the church was given by Jesus "… *you will receive power when the Holy Spirit comes on you; and you will be my witnesses in Jerusalem, and in all Judea and Samaria, and to the ends of the earth.*"(Acts 1:8, NIV) But long before Jesus talked about the ends of the earth, he taught his disciples about the heart of his Father for the whole world. It's a simple phrase that is repeated by billions of people every day, *"your kingdom come, your will be done, on earth as it is in heaven."* (Matthew 6:10, NIV) The early church understood they were commissioned to take the kingdom of heaven to the ends of the earth. For over two thousand years the church has been at that task—sometimes with greater effectiveness than others.

Today we live with the reality that the mission of the church happens simultaneously on two fronts—we continue to go the ends of the earth, while at the same time, with the increase in globalization we find the ends of the earth at our doorstep. We *Go Global* by sending missionaries, partnering with the international church, and by reaching those from other cultures who now find their home with us.

Free Methodist World Missions strategically carries the mission of Jesus in these three avenues: Sending Pioneering Missionaries, Partnering with the International Church, and Reaching Cross Culturally in the United States. This book is divided into three sections, according to that strategy. In the first section, David Roller, a bishop of the Free Methodist Church

USA, writes about sending pioneering missionaries to the ends of the earth. He deals with the field, the funding, and the call of people to go to where there is no testimony of the gospel. In the second section, Linda Adams, Director of International Child Care Ministries, writes about the strategic opportunities in partnering with the international church. As of today, the Free Methodist Church USA comprises about 5% of the World Free Methodist Church. In the third section, Gerald Coates, Director of Global Church Advocacy for Free Methodist World Missions, looks at ways to engage those of different cultures living among us, with special emphasis on reaching the immigrant population.

The challenge is not in seeing the need, but in responding to the call. The call is not just for those who are pioneering the work. The call extends to every member of the body of Christ everywhere. Every disciple of Jesus has received the call to go to the ends of the earth. Every believer in the resurrected Christ is to be engaged in seeing God's kingdom to come and His will to be done on earth, as it is in heaven. The target audience of this book is the North American Christian. Though we make up about 5% of the worldwide church membership, we are stewards of the vast majority of financial resources. We have a special responsibility to separate ourselves from the call of cultural materialism and engage all available resources for the advance of the kingdom.

SECTION 1

PIONEER MISSIONARIES
- David Roller

GOING TO SEA

I was explaining to my granddaughter how, in the old days, many young people went to sea. Some went for adventure but many went for work. That led to explaining about whaling. She didn't like it that people killed whales. Granted. But that led to explaining a world before electric lights.

"Way back, about when your great-great-grandfather was born, people didn't have light bulbs in their houses. Instead they had little pots of oil with a cloth wick and that is how they had light after the sun went down. Can you imagine that? Little lamps burning in your house instead of light bulbs? But do you know where the best oil came from for those lamps? From whales!"

She still didn't think it nice for those people to kill whales. Couldn't get her off that. Even though nobody burns oil lamps anymore. They're a thing of the past. Relics.

When the classic missionaries of the 19th century began to go from Europe and America, they went by sea. There was no other way to get to the people they wanted to get to. A significant part of being "sent" is that missionaries "go." Of course, today they don't need to go by sailing ships; they don't literally "go to sea," but the same idea permeates all of missions—missionaries go.

What's a good definition of a missionary?
What are the essential elements?

When Paul writes to the Italians living in Rome he exudes this eagerness to go:

> I long to see you so that I may impart to you some spiritual gift to make you strong— that is, that you and I may be mutually encouraged by each other's faith. I do not want you to be unaware, brothers and sisters, that I planned many times to come to you (but have been prevented from doing so until now) in order that I might have a harvest among you, just as I have had among the other Gentiles. I am obligated both to Greeks and non-Greeks, both to the wise and the foolish. That is why I am so eager to preach the gospel also to you who are in Rome. (Romans 1:11-15)

Paul is both obligated to go and eager to go. There is this careful combination in the calling of God that combines the magnitude of the task (obligation) with a disposition to fulfill the task (longing and eagerness).

Can you recall any "missionaries" in the Bible who ministered to different people-groups but without leaving home?

Missionaries often go young. If you happen to take a cruise ship to the lovely island of St. Thomas, you may notice one of the three Moravian churches on this small island. In the history of missions those little Moravian churches have a special significance because they're the result of the missionary work begun by two young German men named Leonard Dober and David Nitschmann. One was a potter, and one was a carpenter. They were strong Christians, but no Protestants up to that time had organized any kind of missionary effort. This was back in 1732, well before the beginning of the Great Century of Missions that started in 1796.

Leonard and David didn't sense their missionary calling until an ex-slave, named Anthoy Ulrich, from the Caribbean, spread the word that the African slaves in the Caribbean would be receptive to the gospel. That is, it hadn't occurred to them to be missionaries until they became aware of the need and that they could fill the need. Missionaries usually discover their calling in that same way; there comes an "aha" moment when they can see how the way God made them dovetails neatly with a particular opportunity or calling. Just like the apostle Paul, for Leonard and David there was a crossroads where obligation met eagerness. And they went.

> **If a calling to be a missionary often includes an awareness of the need, what could be done to highlight for young Christians the worldwide need for Jesus?**

Leonard and David left the Moravian community called Herrnhut (in Germany) to walk to Denmark and then to "go to sea," heading toward the Caribbean islands. They were the VERY FIRST organized Protestant missionaries. The Herrnhut community that validated their calling was led by Count Zinzendorf, the nobleman who so influenced John Wesley's theology. And, as suggested earlier, they were young. Leonard Dober was 26 when he sailed for St. Thomas.

He was not unique in being a young missionary. It seems that young adult Christians are those most likely to follow the Lord's call to missions. Perhaps they're less bound by commitments and family; perhaps they're simply less risk-averse; but the examples are striking. Look at the following list of young pioneer missionaries; some are names you might recognize, others are more obscure, but they played significant roles in taking the name of Jesus around the world:

James Hudson Taylor was 21 when he went to China; but over the course of 51 years his ministry directly resulted in some 18,000 conversions.

Amy Carmichael was 22 when she went first to Japan, then India, where she heroically worked rescuing young girls forced into temple prostitution until she died at 83.

William Carey was 32 when he went to Kolkata; but after 41 consecutive years in India, his team had translated the entire Bible into India's 6 major languages.

Inspired by Carey, David Livingston was 27 when he went to southern Africa, tirelessly searching the rest of his life for alternatives to the African-on-African slave trade.

David Brainerd was 25 when he began his ministry to the Native Americans of New Jersey. He died 4 years later, but his writings inspired generations of youthful missionaries.

Adoniram Judson was 25 when he went to Burma; 37 years later he left behind over 100 churches and 8,000 believers.

Jim Elliot was 25 when he left for Ecuador; 4 years later his life ended tragically on a sandbar as he and colleagues made initial contact with the Huaorani people. Their deaths opened the door to decades of fruitful ministry in the jungle.

Jesus was 30 when he began his ministry among the Semitic people of the Middle East, being killed three years later; his death opening the door to eternal life for all of creation!

Missionaries all. They all went, they all traveled (although Brainerd and Jesus went to people-groups near them). They were all young and inexperienced. None of them had done anything of substance up to that point (except Jesus, but that's a little different). They all had the Spirit's fire within that couldn't be banked.

I guess the question is, have young missionaries gone the way of the oil lamp? Are they obsolete? Relics? Has the world and human nature changed so much that young people can no longer be qualified until they're proven church planters, professors, or entrepreneurs?

> *Some of the chapters of this book will explore the fruitfulness of international missionaries. Why might God still want us to "go," rather than simply partnering with international missionaries?*

Or do the waves of the sea still roll? Do mothers and fathers still put their children to bed, tired to the core and hopeless? Do old people still die without a knowledge of their loving creator? Do tribes and nations still go to war because of evil in their hearts? Do women and men still tear apart their marriages? I'm guessing the answer is yes.

As long as the peoples of the world are under the hypnotic curse of sin, we can be sure that God is sending His people to tell them that the curse has been broken; that we can find freedom through Jesus; that the Good News is for them!

> **Given the potential of an able-bodied retirement, what factors would argue in favor of, or against, retirees (rather than just young people) going as missionaries?**

This is why missionaries go. This is why missionaries are not relics. This is why missionaries are needed today all around the globe. Later on in Romans, the apostle Paul reminds us, using the words of Isaiah, of this beautiful task, this beautiful calling:

> How, then, can they call on the one they have not believed in? And how can they believe in the one of whom they have not heard? And how can they hear without someone preaching to them? And how can anyone preach unless they are sent? As it is written: "How beautiful are the feet of those who bring good news!" (Romans 10:14-15)

> **Have you ever sensed the hand of God gently pushing you toward missions? What happened?**

And yet, the world is complex. In spite of Paul's soaring rhetoric, we recognize that the realities of the first century are not the realities of the 18th century, nor the realities of the 21st century. For instance, young people today, who might have considered going as missionaries, are often carrying staggering student loans. They can't see a pathway to ethically abandon those responsibilities to move abroad as missionaries.

> **How might school debt deter twenty-somethings and thirty-somethings from going as missionaries?**

There has also been a de-coupling of Christianity and the concept of "progress" that used to exist. During the Great Century of Missions, the missionary-sending countries were more advanced in their technology (think of medicine, transportation, communication) than the mission-receiving countries. The downside of this was that Christianity was linked to colonialism; the upside was that to become a Christian was to become a modern person. In many ways, becoming a Christian was taking a step of progress toward the future.

> **During the "Great Century of Missions" (the 19th century), missionaries were typically going from which technologically advanced countries?**

All of this makes the point that responding to a call from God to be a missionary today carries much more historic "baggage" than it would have in the 18th century, and is also less attractive, in a cultural sense, than it would have been then.

They will be noble and courageous men and women who today become aware of the need (obligation), and whose hearts leap toward the challenge (eagerness) of preaching the good news to those who have not heard.

> **On a scale of 1 to 10, how eager are you to "go"?**

Jonah, the quintessential missionary in the Old Testament, understood the obligation part, but never became eager to preach in Nineveh. In fact, he had to spend a little time in a great fish before he would even accept God's missionary call on his life. I know the Bible doesn't say the great fish was a whale, but it might have been. If it was a whale it would bolster my standing with my granddaughter; she'd like it if God used a whale to help a missionary go to sea.

Questions for Further Reflection:

1. What's a good definition of a missionary? What are the essential elements?

2. Can you recall any "missionaries" in the Bible, who ministered to different people groups, but without leaving home?

3. If a calling to be a missionary often includes an awareness of the needs, what could be done to highlight, for young Christians, the worldwide need for Jesus?

4. Given the potential of an able-bodied retirement, what factors would argue in favor of, and against, retirees (rather than just young people) going as missionaries?

5. How might school-debt deter 20-somethings and 30-somethings from going as missionaries?

6. During the Great Century of Missions (the 19ᵗʰ century), missionaries were typically going from which technologically-advanced countries?

7. Some chapters of this book will explore the fruitfulness of international missionaries; why might God still want us to go rather than just being funding partners for international missionaries?

8. There are interesting connections between the Moravians and John Wesley. Can you discover any in America, in their transatlantic crossings, and on continental Europe?

9. Have you ever sensed the hand of God gently pushing you toward missions? What happened?

10. On a scale of 1-10, how eager are you to "go"?

THE FINANCES

I (David) was twenty years old and just married for four weeks when I was invited to apply for a job in Spain. Yvonne and I had no great job prospects and fewer plans. We were just enjoying life as newlyweds in our small upstairs apartment in Michigan. The offer in Spain seemed exotic and interesting, especially compared to our little town. The college that was offering the job was going to pay us more than I had ever been paid ($9,200!). Easy decision. We said, "Let's go!"

We didn't go as missionaries to Spain. It was an assignment with a Christian college. But a strange thing happened to us during those 10 months in Spain; our eyes were opened to new possibilities:

> The possibility that most people didn't have access to a church.

> The possibility that people could stand in a huge cathedral yet never hear the Jesus part of the story.

> The possibility that our lives could be spent on something bigger than ourselves.

Those new possibilities led us to seminary, then as Free Methodist missionaries to Mexico. One of our first teams that visited us in Mexico was composed of U.S. college students. They had a good ministry for a week and then went back to college.

But an interesting result came from that trip. A couple of years later, about 1982, having graduated from college, one of those team members wrote us and sent a check, saying he wanted to participate in our ministry. That was great. It wasn't a lot of money, but greatly appreciated. The next month he sent another check. That was wonderful. And then every month after that.

He got married. They sent a check together. They had two children. They sent a check every month. He lost his job. They sent a check. He got a new job. They sent a bigger check. We moved to Chile. They still sent a check. As I write this, 35 years later, they're still sending a monthly check! That's over 400 months in a row. I've never seen anything like it.

They don't want a tax-deductible receipt. They just want to participate in this ministry together with us. What sweet partners.

One of the first to model this partner-relationship between the ministry and those who support the ministry was the Shunammite woman in 2 Kings 4. She is described as well-to-do. Because she is a woman of means, Elisha the prophet would often eat with her and her husband when he passed through Shunem. It occurs to her that Elisha could use a room to sleep in, so she has a room built for him and furnishes it so he can be comfortable in his ministry. One day Elisha arrives, stretches out on the bed, and while he's lying there, he wonders how he can repay her—he wants to reward her for her participation in his ministry.

Elisha promises her she'll have a son, and sure enough, within the year she and her husband have a child. Eventually the son gets sick and dies but is brought back to life by Elisha. The relationship between the prophet and the woman who supports him is the key part of the story. We realize that her financial support means she is woven into his ministry.

Jesus may be referencing the Shunammite woman in Matthew 10 when he says, "Anyone who welcomes you welcomes me, and anyone who welcomes me welcomes the one who sent me. Whoever welcomes a prophet as a prophet will receive a prophet's reward, and whoever welcomes a righteous person as a righteous person will receive a righteous person's reward. And if anyone gives even a cup of cold water to one of these little ones who is my disciple, truly I tell you, that person will certainly not lose their reward." (Matthew 10:40-42)

> *Given Jesus' words in Matthew 10, above, it appears that God sees and takes note of even the smallest gift. How might we build giving habits into our children's lives?*

Jesus is talking about rewards; the rewards will be for what we have done. As Protestants, we're quick to avoid the trap of works-righteousness. We know that we are not saved by our good works. We're saved by our relationship with God through our Lord Jesus. But that relationship will be evidenced by our goodness. Our goodness should be evident to all.

And that goodness, that welcoming and giving, unifies us with the ones we welcome and those to whom we give. By giving we become part of the foundation that bears the weight of the ministry. The ministry crashes without that foundation.

> *Do you think it's better to support one ministry heavily or spread out your contributions?*
>
> *Since the Free Methodist Church uses annual commitments to build a trustworthy support system for missionaries, do you use that system?*

Let's imagine a missionary who decides to "go global" and to accept a pioneer missionary assignment. That missionary will need to engage many financial supporters as partners in ministry or they will not be able to go. Those financial supporters, then, are what makes the ministry possible! That's why they participate in the rewards—because they are participating in the ministry.

> *How does altruism (giving without receiving) connect with this idea of participating in a prophet's reward? In other words, if altruism is eventually rewarded, does that make it less altruistic?*

Because of this, I will confess to having a selfish, scheming thought as a missionary. More than once, during our missionary years, I thought, "I'd go home in a heartbeat and support somebody else to become a missionary. After all, if I can get in on the reward and yet stay comfortably at home... why stay here?" But even as I thought it, I remembered that we weren't there for the "reward"—our reward was in seeing transformed lives. But the thought was there.

> **How do you feel when you receive a missionary's request to support her or his ministry?**

The true reality behind this "prophet's reward" concept is the importance of a ministry's financial supporters. Those who give to send a missionary are not second-tier spectators—they are mission-critical participants. Although, admittedly, some are more mission-critical than others!

> **What advantages can you think of for giving to missionaries that your own denomination sends, rather than missionaries sponsored by other organizations? What disadvantages might there be?**

Let's think about giving gifts to people for a moment, to help us understand our giving to support ministry. The best gifts meet two criteria: 1) they cost the giver something and 2) they connect with what the recipient values.

> **What's the gift you've most enjoyed giving? What makes it stand out?**

Great gifts cost us something: A great gift will be on a level commensurate with the giver's economy. While a three-year-old's great gift might be a crayon drawing, if an adult tries to give a crayon drawing, it's obvious that their heart's not in it. Great gifts impact the giver's own economy.

Great gifts also connect with the recipient's values: Just spending a lot of money isn't enough to make it a great gift. A great gift also shows I understand you; what you care about, what you dream about.

> **Thinking of a missionary you support, what's a special gift you could give them that demonstrates you understand the things they value?**

If we apply those principles to our ministry-giving, we begin to understand why Jesus says "a cup of cold water" will be rewarded. In the right circumstances ("to one of these little ones who is my disciple") that cup of cold water could be a huge gift. In other circumstances, it could be an insult. What did the cup of cold water cost me? And how much was it needed? Cost and values are the two principles.

> **Don't share this answer with others, but what size gift, for you, classifies it as a "great gift" that costs you something? $10,000? $200? $1,000?**

The Philippian believers understood all this intuitively. The Apostle Paul writes an effusive, joyful letter to them, in part because they have sent him some financial support. Paul rejoices that they have not forgotten him but have sent him gifts several times. But even as he's thanking them, he's recognizing that, by their gifts, they have become participants in his ministry. Beyond that, part of his joy is because their giving is actually benefiting them, as well as him. "Not that I desire your gifts; what I desire is that more be credited to your account." (Philippians 4:17). Paul certainly is not talking about a bank account, but in some sense, he is recognizing the same thing Elisha saw and that Jesus referenced; there is a benefit to giving.

> **Who is your favorite Biblical example of a financial giver?**

Putting this in the vernacular, there's a "double-dip" for those who give to enable ministry: 1) their participation in the ministry enables the good work to be done; and 2) their own account is increased.

Won't it be a delight to stand in front of God's eternal throne, to see Him high and lifted up? And then, to see the stately procession of faithful servants who through the millennia have given themselves to ministry in Jesus' name? Won't we applaud and cheer their sacrifices and pure motivation? Won't we whistle and cry as their stories are told and they receive their rewards? And won't we be amazed as those who faithfully gave, month after month, take their place beside them? Thousands upon thousands, who never went, but who sent. Tens of thousands who purposefully, and with long-term commitment, denied themselves and gave sacrificially. Givers, who gave in line with their ability and who valued what God values. Participants, every one.

Questions for Further Reflection:

1. What's the gift you've most enjoyed giving? What makes it stand out?

2. Who is your favorite Biblical example of a financial giver?

3. Don't share this answer with others, but, what size gift, for you, classifies it as a "great gift" that costs you something? $10,000? $200? $1,000?

4. How do you feel when you receive a missionary's request to support her or his ministry?

5. Do you think it's better to support one ministry heavily, or spread out your contributions?

6. What advantages can you think of for giving to missionaries that your own denomination sends, rather than missionaries sponsored by other organizations? What disadvantages might there be?

7. How does altruism (giving without receiving) connect with this idea of participating in a prophet's reward? In other words, if altruism is eventually rewarded, does that make it less altruistic?

8. Given Jesus' words in Matthew 10, above, it appears that God sees and takes note of even the smallest gift. How might we build giving habits into our children's lives?

9. Since the Free Methodist Church uses annual commitments to build a trustworthy support system for missionaries, do you use that system?

10. Thinking of a missionary you support, what's a special gift you could give them that demonstrates you understand the things they value?

NEED NOT APPLY?

You might think that after two thousand years, the task of carrying the gospel to the ends of the earth should be done. And perhaps it would be, if new people weren't constantly being born! But every new generation must begin anew to fulfill the great commission. We can't say, for instance, "Latin America is now Christian," because following Jesus is a dynamic relationship, not a pin in a map. No area of the world is ever "Christian" and checked off the to-do list.

Because of this, every generation inherits the great commission's mandate to send their own missionaries to testify of the goodness of God poured out to the whole world through his son, Jesus, the Christ; some go to places filled with churches and genuine faith, others to places filled with churches that are merely relics, while yet others go to places where the name of Jesus has never been heard.

> *How did the good news of Jesus come to you?*
> *Missionaries were involved, even if in the distant past,*
> *but do you know who they were? In other words, how*
> *did the Gospel reach you?*

We have been using the term "Pioneer Missionary" but have not yet defined it. The word "Pioneer" may bring to mind hatchets, log cabins and Conestoga wagons. But when we talk about pioneer missionaries, we simply mean missionaries who open new territory, whether geographic, cultural or ethnic. In that sense, they are pioneers.

In contrast with pioneer missionaries, most missionaries are sent to work with the established church in international settings. Some may be church planters or evangelists, but usually the missionaries who work with the international church are in training and educational roles, providing support for international leaders. This is very fruitful work, and we'll look at this more in following chapters. But any comprehensive long-term strategy must include pioneer missionaries who are moving into new places and new people groups.

> **What do you understand to be the main differences between pioneer missionaries and missionaries who work with the international church?**

If you were to send a pioneer missionary, where would you send them? To the most fruitful places and people? Or to the places and people that are least reached? Or would you look for places and people that perhaps have some witness to the gospel but very little in common with our Wesleyan understanding of Scripture?

The Christian church has not had a unified response to those questions. Nor has there been a master strategy for spreading the good news of Jesus. There have been conferences that have divided up the world and assigned mission responsibilities (like the 1910 World Missionary Conference in Edinburgh), but it has usually been through missionaries, like Leonard Dober and David Nitschmann, who moved out toward unpredictable and unplanned opportunities.

> **Are you the kind of person who's more inclined to financially support a pioneer missionary or a missionary connected to the international church?**

The church expanded in the book of Acts in much the same way the church expands today, spontaneously and organically, not by following some Gantt chart of lineal expectations. Four critical moments which transformed the Christ followers from a Jewish sect to a global movement are chronicled in the book of Acts: the day of Pentecost, Peter's visit to the gentile Cornelius, the first missionaries to Antioch, and Paul's decision to go to Rome. These are the key moments when the church broke out of its boundaries and spilled over into new places and new people groups. These are moments of pioneering new territory.

The third of those is Acts 11:23

> Some of them, however, men from Cyprus and Cyrene, went to Antioch and began to speak to Greeks also, telling them the good news about the Lord Jesus. The Lord's hand was with them, and a great number of people believed and turned to the Lord.
> (Acts 11:20-21)

These unnamed "men from Cyprus and Cyrene" couldn't contain their enthusiasm to share the good news about Jesus. Apparently, without writing any white papers or convening any boards, they just started sharing the good news with Greeks, who responded and turned to the Lord. This was a major advance because until then, no one expected faith among the Greeks. Everyone assumed Jesus was a Jewish messiah, that Christianity was a Jewish phenomenon; limited good news for the people of God.

But then these unnamed men become unwitting pioneer missionaries. They perfectly illustrate what pioneer missionaries do—they go to new places or new peoples with the good news. Pioneer missionaries cross the boundaries of geography or language or culture without a hosting church to receive them on the other side of that boundary.

> *Can you identify any people groups living around you for whom a missionary would need to cross a language barrier? A cultural barrier?*

The fourth of those key moments in Acts when the church moved into new places and peoples is at the end of Paul's ministry in Ephesus in chapter 19.

After all this had happened, Paul decided to go to Jerusalem, passing through Macedonia and Achaia. "After I have been there," he said, "I must visit Rome also." (Acts 19:21)

Paul is experiencing tremendous success in his two years of ministry in Ephesus. But he recognizes the need to get to Rome. Rome is the cultural, civic, and military capital of the western world. Consequently, Paul strategically targets the center of the majority culture, "I must visit Rome." This is pioneer missionary work because, although there are already Christians in Rome, there is not yet a significant indigenous church. So Paul turns his face toward Rome, making the jump from the Greek world to the Roman world and from the edges of the culture to the center of the culture.

> *How might we imitate the Apostle Paul's decision to turn toward Rome and the majority culture?*
>
> *Rather than turning toward the majority culture as missionaries, what other kinds of reactions do you see Christians having toward the majority culture?*

The church usually sends missionaries more like Acts chapter 11 than Acts chapter 19. As in chapter 11, following networks of people and contacts, the church is constantly probing the world's areas for receptivity to the good news of Jesus. Different areas of the globe become receptive to the wind of the Spirit at different times. Perhaps due to a change in government or following a natural disaster or war, or when a population becomes disenchanted with their belief system, people groups become responsive to the good news. When that responsiveness is detected, pioneer missionaries move in to live among the people.

> *Of the following three options which would be your priority for the placing pioneer missionaries?*
>
> *a) to the most fruitful places and people?*
> *b) to the least-reached places and people?*
> *c) to the places and people without a "Wesleyan witness?"*

But sending is not usually done in a corporate way, with charts and graphs and scientific gadgets that detect "evangelistic responsiveness." Instead, what usually happens is that pioneer missionaries go to places that are NOT responsive. They move in. They follow Jesus' model of living among the people to whom they are sent. They learn the language of the people. They learn about their beliefs, assumptions, and values. They love those to whom they are sent. This may take years, decades even. These kinds of pioneer missionaries are our detectors of evangelistic responsiveness. They are how the rest of the world will know when that people group becomes responsive.

> *Are you aware of any missionaries who are this kind of persistent missionary who's in it for the long haul?*

For example, a Free Methodist layman, Samuel E. Mills, went to the Dominican Republic in 1889 as a lay missionary. He was the first missionary of any denomination to minister to the Spanish-speaking population of the island. He was there for seven years before he saw his first convert! But today there are over 27,000 Free Methodists in that country. The church wouldn't have developed as it has without his pioneering spirit.

> *If you had been Samuel Mills, why wouldn't you have returned home after 4, or 5, or 6 years of fruitless ministry? What might have kept him in the Dominican Republic during those years?*

Pioneer missionaries often go to places that are not currently fruitful. Pioneer missionaries are patient. Pioneer missionaries are willing to invest in long-term potential; they don't demand quick results. Sometimes, pioneer missionaries have spectacular success, like the Apostle Paul, but more often their ministry is like that of Priscilla and Aquila (co-laborers with Paul who helped consolidate his ministry efforts by following his ministry path): steady-as-she-goes.

Pioneer missionaries may also have a public relations challenge, since their work is often in less receptive territory than that of missionaries who work with the established church in the host country. Compare for a moment the newsletters of Priscilla and Aquila with the Apostle Paul's newsletter. Which would have been more exciting and motivating? While Paul would have been writing of shipwrecks, snakebites and mass conversions, Priscilla and Aquila would have written, "When Priscilla and Aquila heard him (Apollos), they invited him to their home and explained to him the way of God more adequately." (Acts 18:26). Yet both ministries are valid and necessary. Both are worthy of our lives. Apply now.

Questions for Further Reflection:

1. How did the good news of Jesus come to you? Missionaries were involved, even if in the distant past, but do you know who they were? In other words, how did the Gospel reach you?

   Carolyn Winslow, missionary to China but WWII brought her back to USA where she kept up her child evangelism efforts (even in Lakeview, MI)

2. What do you understand to be the main differences between pioneer missionaries and missionaries who work with the international church?

3. Are you the kind of person who's more inclined to go as a pioneer missionary or as a missionary connected to the international church?

4. Can you identify any people groups living around you for whom a missionary would need to cross a language barrier? A cultural barrier?

5. Are you the kind of person who's more inclined to financially support a pioneer missionary or a missionary connected to the international church?

6. How might we imitate the Apostle Paul's decision to turn toward Rome and the majority culture?

7. Rather than turning toward the majority culture as missionaries, what other kinds of reactions do you see Christians having toward the majority culture?

8. Of the following three options, which would be your priority for the placing of pioneer missionaries?
    a) to the most fruitful places and people?
    b) to the least-reached places and people?
    c) to the places and people without a "Wesleyan witness?"

9. Are you aware of any missionaries who are this kind of persistent missionary, who are in it for the long haul?

10. If you had been Samuel Mills, why wouldn't you have returned home after 4, or 5, or 6 years of fruitless ministry? What might have kept him in the Dominican Republic during those years?

PAST, PRESENT, YOU

There are about 7.4 billion people in the world. According to the researchers at the Joshua project, over 3 billion of them are unreached with the good news of Jesus. By unreached we mean there is no "indigenous, self-sustaining disciple-making Christian movement among their people group." This is just under 40% of the world's population! That's why pioneer missionaries are still needed.

> *There are reasons why those 3 billion unreached people, alive today, are still unreached with the good news. Can you conjecture or research what those reasons might be? In other words, what are the barriers that must be crossed to reach them?*

The challenge is complicated by the fact that these unreached people groups are often sealed off; there are not many natural bridges, even from their own compatriots, because they are from other people groups. Think of how hard it would be for you to effectively minister to the Puebloan people living in New Mexico, even though you're both Americans and both living in the same country. Perhaps less obvious but just as great would be the differences between a northern mestizo Mexican and the 48% of the Mexicans in the state of Oaxaca that belong to the 16 different ethnic groups in that state. They're all Mexican citizens, but the gospel will not naturally flow from one to the other. Different languages, different cultures, different geography.

The size of the opportunity (3 billion unreached opportunities!) coupled with the complexities of the opportunity demonstrate the potential and necessity of sending both western and non-western pioneer missionaries.

But the US church, in all its expressions, is seeing a marked decrease in the sending of missionaries, perhaps best illustrated by the decline of 1000 Southern Baptist missionaries reported in 2016.[1] This appears to be due to multiple trends, including: a theological retreat from the concept of eternal punishment or separation from goodness (Hell), anti-immigration and anti-Muslimism, high student debt, short-term horizon for results, and increased concern about well-intentioned but ineffective missional activity.

Ironically then, at a time when new tools such as the internet and cheap air travel are making missions ever more effective, interest is waning in missions. But missions is such a central theme of God's story that it cannot be minimized in the life of the Christian.

> *The church failed to communicate a theology of missions and a missiology (how missions should be done) in ways that move Christians into missions.*
>
> *How might this be better done?*
> *How might your local church do this better?*

Messenger People

The story of missions is so thoroughly embedded in the biblical story that without it, we would have no Bible. We would have no Bible if we extracted the parts about God engaging with His special messenger-people, because this is the story of the Bible: a loving God, rejected by his creation, wooing his creation back to His embrace by means of a covenant messenger people. That wooing of the whole world through a covenant people is what we call missions. It's that simple and that central to the story.

---

1 Zylstra, Sarah Eekhoff, "Southern Baptists Lose Almost 1,000 Missionaries as IMB Cuts Costs," *Christianity Today*, Feb. 24, 2016, http://www.christianitytoday.com/news/2016/february/southern-baptists-lose-1132-missionaries-staff-imb-cuts.html, accessed June 5, 2017.

It began with the Trinity, that perfect union, that perfect relationship. With the utterance of a word that perfect relationship expanded to include the creation. But it all went wrong when the creation lifted its fist in rebellion, rejecting the creator's good plan. The smear of consequence dragged its contagious stain through the pages of history until Jesus inserted himself in our history, lifted the curse, and reconciled us to our true family of origin. Through the whole story, the unified godhead courts his creation with acts of loving kindness and sends those who respond on mission, to those who have yet to respond. This is the mission that results in missions: obedient joyful participation with God to bring all things into proper relationship.

That synopsis isn't nearly as interesting as the Bible, because God didn't choose to write a textbook on theology, instead he chose to record the stories of men and women as they succeeded and failed in their participation in that mission.

> *Why might God have given us a Bible full of stories of men and women succeeding and failing, instead of a theological textbook?*
>
> *What are the benefits and disadvantages of that?*

This big story of missions breaks down into these major components:

Before Abraham: After the flood, Noah is told to scatter and inhabit the whole earth (Genesis 9). In disobedience, some chose to build the Tower of Babel, rather than be scattered (Genesis 11).

Abraham's family as the missionary people: God calls Terah to journey with him to a country of promise (Genesis 11). Terah's son, Abraham, is subsequently called by God to continue that journey and to establish the people of God through whom *all* the nations will be blessed (Genesis 12). Abraham and Sarah's descendants, the Hebrews, are the chosen ones, the missionary people. They are called into this special covenant with God, not just for themselves, but as the agents of restoration and reconciliation for *all* peoples.

This family, the Israelites, fail as the missionary people, but with occasional examples of understanding. Several times, other people groups are "grafted" into the family of God:

- Rahab in Jericho (Joshua 2).
- The prophets (Elijah, Elisha) reveal God as the God of all, not just of the Hebrews (see especially Namaan and the widow of Zarephath).
- Ruth, the Moabite becomes the great-grandmother of King David.
- David, in the Psalms, proclaims the universality of God over all peoples.
- Jonah is the best example of an individual missionary in the Old Testament.
- Daniel and friends spread the story of God, even in their captivity.
- The prophets, both major and minor, insist that God is for all the restoration of all the nations.

> *In addition to those mentioned, what other Old Testament stories include a ministry to non-Hebrew people?*

Jesus inhabits the creation to call a new missionary people: Jesus' ministry is clearly to "the lost sheep of Israel." He has come to turn them from their dry traditions to the living God so that they can fulfill their mandate to be a missionary people. But even as he focuses on Israel, Jesus clearly has a global scope. For instance, Luke records Jesus' dramatic homecoming to Nazareth that begins with adulation of Jesus when he reminds them of Isaiah 61. That chapter affirms the extraordinary nature of the Jewish people, even promising that immigrants and foreigners will do their farm work for them (Isaiah 61:5). But then Jesus challenges his hometown with the universal nature of the gospel by reminding them that Elijah and Elisha ministered to foreigners. The crowd swiftly turns on Jesus, and, in a murderous mood, tries to throw Jesus off a cliff. All this from a crowd supposedly rooting for the local boy made good!

God's great gift to us at Christmas is reflected and multiplied in your wonderful giving to bless his children all over the world. Thanks so much for standing with International Child Care Ministries in 2017.

A Blessed Christmas!

Linda Adams

> *The radical change of mood in Jesus' ministry in Nazareth in Luke 4 is clearly provoked by the two stories about Naaman and the widow of Zarephath. Why might this have so angered his neighbors? Do you ever see that kind of anger about foreigners today?*

In the twelfth chapter of John something happens that serves as the "trigger" for Jesus to "go global!" When the Greeks (foreigners) want to see Jesus, the focus turns to the global redemption story. After the resurrection, the church slowly begins to understand that they are the new missionary people—the true offspring of Abraham—and are therefore responsible for carrying the good news to those who have not heard.

> *In addition to those mentioned, what other incidents in the life of Jesus include a ministry to non-Hebrew people?*

Post-Resurrection: the newly formed church launches out in a missionary movement across the world, crossing linguistic, geographic and cultural barriers that continues to this day.

Are we that people?

This is only the broadest-stroke outline of *the* people on a mission. But it has not been recorded as Holy Scripture to satisfy our idle historical curiosity; it has been recorded to reveal God. Once we understand that the essential nature of God is to embrace, in love, his errant creation through Jesus, via the proclamation of a missionary people, we're confronted with a potentially awkward question: How are we doing? Are we about what God is about? Are we living in obedience?

If God is a missionary God, and if God is looking for a missionary people, are we that people? When they write our story, will it be of a people who went, or of a people who stayed? A people who proclaimed to others, or who kept to themselves? A people who sent people, or a people who collected stuff?

If you're able, research at www.joshuaproject.net *if any of the 48 unreached people groups live in your state. You probably won't have any connections to them (that's why they're unreached!), but you'll begin to see patterns of where they live and where they come from. Is there anything you could do?*

Forty percent of the world's population is unreached with the good news about Jesus. Yet, at the same time, giving by Free Methodists through Free Methodist World Missions to support missionaries (MSA accounts) and national ministries (CSA accounts) averages about $60 per year, per member. That is a staggeringly small amount for a people whose primary task is to participate with God in His plan to save the world! Regardless of what reasons make that amount so small (many of them are undoubtedly good), it's clear that most Free Methodists are not participating wholeheartedly in our international missionary efforts.

We have suggested that there are some good explanations for why only $60 per year per member is given by Free Methodists to our mission's efforts.

What might some of those explanations be?

Take a few moments to poke around the giving site for Free Methodist World Missions at https://give.fmcusa.org/. *Familiarize yourself with the drop-down tabs of Countries and Missionaries. Do any opportunities there pull at your heart?*

The glimpses that John provides us, in the book of Revelation, into what the gathered people of God will look like around the throne is startling in its inclusiveness. That throng really will be from every tribe and tongue. What John saw wasn't only people like himself; he saw people that looked like the breadth of God's good creation. How many of them will be of the 7.4 billion alive right now? How many of the unreached 3 billion might we still reach in our lifetime, so they, too, may gather around that good throne? Love for our good God draws us into his sweet plan to bring wellbeing to everyone. Pioneer missionaries must go today.

Questions for Further Reflection:

1. In addition to those mentioned, what other Old Testament stories include a ministry to non-Hebrew people?

2. In addition to those mentioned, what other incidents in the life of Jesus include a ministry to non-Hebrew people?

3. Why might God have given us a Bible full of stories of men and women succeeding and failing, instead of a theological textbook? What are the benefits and disadvantages of that?

4. The radical change of mood in Jesus' ministry in Nazareth in Luke 4 is clearly provoked by the two stories about Naaman and the widow of Zarephath. Why might this have so angered his neighbors? Do you ever see that kind of anger about foreigners today?

5. There are reasons why those 3 billion unreached people, alive today, are still unreached with the good news. Can you conjecture, or research what those reasons might be? In other words, what are the barriers that must be crossed to reach them?

6. If you're able, research at www.joshuaproject.net if any of the 48 unreached people groups live in your state. You probably won't have any connections to them (that's why they're unreached!), but you'll begin to see patterns of where they live and where they come from. Is there anything you could do?

7. The church failed to communicate a theology of missions and a missiology (how missions should be done) in ways that move Christians into missions. How might this be better done?

8. How might your local church do this better?

9. We have suggested that there are some good explanations for why only $60 per year per member is given by Free Methodists to our mission's efforts. What might some of those explanations be?

10. Take a few moments to poke around the giving site for Free Methodist World Missions at https://give.fmcusa.org/. Familiarize yourself with the drop-down tabs of Countries and Missionaries. Do any opportunities there pull at your heart?

SECTION II

PARTNERING WITH THE INTERNATIONAL CHURCH
- Linda Adams

GOD'S END GAME

We're living in an amazing time in God's unfolding story called the Free Methodist Church. Our global membership is over one million. Of that million, only 5% live in the United States. That means 95% of the family lives in places we once thought of as mission fields or in current mission frontiers. In some parts of the world, growth is breathtakingly rapid!

> *How does your view of the Free Methodist Church shift when you realize that fewer than 5% of our members live in the United States?*

Most of the growth of the church is in the "2/3 World" and is happening because indigenous church planters and missionaries are reaching out to new people groups and geographic regions. It makes sense that Indian missionaries are the ones to carry the Good News to new tribes in India, and African missionaries cross linguistic and national borders to reach other Africans. Latin American believers have sent church planters to work among Spanish and Portuguese speakers in Europe, North America, and across South America. And, yes, God continues to raise up Americans with a passion to pioneer new territories. If we wrapped colored string around a globe to represent all the sending and receiving that's going on, it would look like one big multicolored ball of yarn!

Since we, in what some call "the Mother Church," are now such a tiny minority of our global family, what roles remain for us? For one thing, some of us will still go. Our Missionary God continues to call certain individuals to give their lives to reach the nations. This happens wherever the church is alive to the Spirit. From the Book of Acts until now, a faithful church is a sending church, and some will say, "Here am I, send me."

Do you see evidence that your church believes that God still calls some of his followers here to become missionaries in distant lands? If a person in your church felt that nudge from God, how would he or she be directed to pursue that inner sense of God's call?

But a new role has emerged as the church around the world has become established and mature. We can support our brothers and sisters in their outreach and compassionate ministries and their expansion to new people. Many of our loved ones live in places of profound poverty, where incomes average less than $5 a day. In those economies, our dollars are very valuable, so it makes sense that some of our support is financial. By responsibly working with global partners, we can help to fund leadership development, church planting, and works of mercy that lead to community transformation. The Country Support Accounts (CSA) of Free Methodist World Missions are one channel for this.

Our dollars can be very valuable in other economies. What have you experienced about getting a "bang for your buck" by investing in international leaders or their ministries?

In this spirit of cooperation, we financially assist hospitals, schools, and pastoral training centers. We sponsor children through International Child Care Ministries, investing in their future self-support and currently employing hundreds of adults who lead the children's programs. Through SEED (Sustainable Empowerment through Economic Development) we provide widows and other disadvantaged members of livelihood groups the opportunity to earn a fair wage and feed their families. The Set Free Movement supports initiatives to prevent human trafficking and joins other groups along the continuum of care to provide justice for those who have been exploited. All these forms of financial investment are designed to empower local church leaders to impact their own communities for the better. Our sharing of this financial burden is strategic, leveraging their time and capacities to accomplish more than we could ever do as foreigners.

> *What value do you see in partnering within the denomination for international mercy ministries and development work, as compared with partnering with NGOs and other organizations outside the Free Methodist Church?*
>
> *What ways have you found in your own personal finances to free up resources for those around the world?*

We can also share expertise. For instance, doctors and nurses from the U.S. train nationals in hospitals and clinics in several countries. Professors volunteer to teach courses at emerging universities. Visiting pastors conduct continuing education workshops in countries where seminary has been out of reach for the average church leader. Engineers, electricians, well-drillers, reforestation farmers, computer technicians, plumbers, and construction workers share their skills with workers in other countries so they can ply their trades more effectively. When done well, these efforts build capacity and empower people.

> *How would you say the role of Western missionaries has changed, according to the thrust of this chapter? What have we primarily moved from and what are we moving to?*

Learning to do this well involves navigating the rapids of cross-cultural engagement so both parties are respected and understood, and the whole partnership does a lot of good and minimal harm. It's not easy! Systems can be set up that throw a lot of money at a problem, but instead of solving the problem, make it worse. Attitudes of entitlement and dependency can be formed; frustrations and unfulfilled expectations on both sides can ruin the whole enterprise. Cross-cultural communication for shared development of partnerships is a never-ending learning curve!

The website HonorShame.com provides the following contrasts of "Cultural Vantage Points." The contrasts show how the West and East perceive each other's cultural values:

- In relationships, the West values equality, which seems disrespectful to the East, which values hierarchy. Hierarchy seems oppressive to Westerners.
- In orientation to time, the West's task focus seems unkind to the East, whose event focus seems inconsiderate to people from the West.
- In speech, the West prizes honesty, which seems rude to the East. The East values harmony, which can seem dishonest to the West.
- When it comes to money, the West seeks independence, which seems stingy to the East. The East seeks patronage, which to the West seems corrupt.
- With food, the West values efficiency, which seems neglectful to the East. The East values hospitality, which seems ostentatious to the West.
- Ethics in the West are guilt-based, which seems shameless to the East. The East's ethics are shame-based, which seems lawless to the West.

> *Discuss these contrasting cultural value points between East and West. Have you experienced any tensions in cross-cultural relationships that can be understood by this set of contrasts?*
>
> *Where in your study of God's Word have you seen eastern cultural values that challenge your western ideals? How do Jesus' parables challenge your cultural values?*

If all this is true, how can we possibly hope to work together and accomplish anything? The Church in the Book of Acts navigated these waters long before us. Beginning with Jesus' words in Acts 1:8 that his followers would be his witnesses in "Jerusalem, Judea, Samaria and to the ends of the earth," boundaries were crossed and cultures both cooperated and clashed. The beautiful and fascinating journey of the Early Church recorded in Acts encounters many cross-cultural challenges.

For instance, the Day of Pentecost foreshadowed the missionary frontiers of the Church as Jewish speakers of every language in the known world heard the message in their own tongue (Acts 2:5-13). As the believers in Jerusalem shared material goods, Greek-speaking widows were neglected in favor of Hebrew-speaking widows (Acts 6:1). The solution was to select a cross-cultural team of deacons to handle the distribution of food.

Philip crossed the religious barrier to evangelize in Samaria (Acts 9:5-8). Next, he conversed with a eunuch from Ethiopia, who received the Good News, was baptized, and returned to his home rejoicing in newfound faith (Acts 9:26-39). The Apostle Peter and a Roman centurion named Cornelius experienced uncanny parallel visions; their chapter ends with this God-fearing Gentile and his family receiving the gift of the Holy Spirit (Acts 10:44-48). From there, the story of the gospel bringing diverse people into unity goes on and on, until the present day.

> *How do the situations described here from the early chapters of Acts illustrate that cross-cultural challenges have always been with us?*

Always in the back of our minds is the Book of Revelation's glorious picture of Jesus the Lamb, surrounded by worshipping multitudes from every people group in scenes like this: "And they sang a new song, saying, 'Worthy are you to take the scroll and to open its seals, for you were slain and by your blood you ransomed people for God from every tribe and language and people and nation...'" (Revelation 5:9). This is God's end-game, the goal toward which all of history is leaning. Nothing should inspire us more than to know that we'll be included in this great throng, and nothing should motivate us more than to know we can participate in God's great global work so that others will be there, too.

> *What steps can you take now to prepare yourself for the rich diversity of God's family that's portrayed in Revelation?*

Questions for Further Reflection:

1. How does your view of the Free Methodist Church shift when you realize that fewer than 5% of our members live in the United States?

2. Do you see evidence that your church believes that God still calls some of his followers here to become missionaries in distant lands? If a person in your church felt that nudge from God, how would he or she be directed to pursue that inner sense of God's call?

3. The author claims that our dollars can be very valuable in other economies. What have you experienced about getting a "bank for your buck" by investing in international leaders or their ministries?

4. What value do you see in partnering within the denomination for international mercy ministries and development work, as compared with partnering with NGOs and other organizations outside the Free Methodist Church?

5. How would you say the role of Western missionaries has changed, according to the thrust of this chapter? What have we primarily moved from and what are we moving to?

6. Discuss the contrasting cultural value points between East and West listed in the chapter. Have you experienced any tensions in cross-cultural relationships that can be understood by this set of contrasts?

7. Where in your study of God's Word have you seen eastern cultural values that challenge your western ideals? How do Jesus' parables challenge your cultural values?

8. How do the situations described here from the early chapters of Acts illustrate that cross-cultural challenges have always been with us?

9. What ways have you found in your own personal finances to free up resources for those around the world?

10. What steps can you take now to prepare yourself for the rich diversity of God's family that's portrayed in Revelation?

SILVER AND GOLD MIGHT BE NICE

When I was a teenager, my favorite part in the whole Bible was the paragraph at the end of Acts Chapter 2 that describes the Early Church's inclusive community:

They devoted themselves to the apostles' teaching and to fellowship, to the breaking of bread and to prayer. Everyone was filled with awe at the many wonders and signs performed by the apostles. All the believers were together and had everything in common. They sold property and possessions to give to anyone who had need. Every day they continued to meet together in the temple courts. They broke bread in their homes and ate together with glad and sincere hearts, praising God and enjoying the favor of all the people. And the Lord added to their number daily those who were being saved. (Acts 2:42-47)

This sounded like perfection. I had enjoyed the privilege of experiencing a church in an extended revival, and we had tasted an appetizer of what this feast of love and unity in the Body of Christ must have been like. To me, the Early Church lived the dream: intense immersion in teaching and corporate prayer; miraculous healings; open-handed sharing of possessions so that nobody would be left in need. Communal meals, glad hearts, joyful worship, sincere praise, and generous love stunned a watching world. What could be more convincing and attractive to outsiders? Every single day more people joined this community of radical love.

> *Have you ever "tasted an appetizer" of the kind of community described in Acts 2:42-47? Tell us about it.*

> *If your church started a practice where people sold possessions and shared them with the poor members of the church, what concerns would you have?*
>
> *How much do you think the community around your church building knows about your church? If they know you're there, does anything about your church appeal to them?*
>
> *Have you ever wondered, "Did some of the people who joined the movement do it just to get the possessions that were being shared?" Maybe.*

The very next scene in the story involves a beggar who had been lame from birth asking Peter and John for money.

> Peter looked straight at him, as did John. Then Peter said, "Look at us!" So the man gave them his attention, expecting to get something from them. Then Peter said, "Silver or gold I do not have, but what I do have I give you. In the name of Jesus Christ of Nazareth, walk." Taking him by the right hand, he helped him up, and instantly the man's feet and ankles became strong. He jumped to his feet and began to walk. Then he went with them into the temple courts, walking and jumping, and praising God. When all the people saw him walking and praising God, they recognized him as the same man who used to sit begging at the temple gate called Beautiful, and they were filled with wonder and amazement at what had happened to him. (Acts 3:4b-10)

The man expected to get money from them. It was the most he could hope for, the greatest response he could imagine. A few coins in his cup would get him through another day. But Peter shocked him by looking him in the eye and saying, "Silver or gold I do not have, but what I do have I give you. In the name of Jesus Christ of Nazareth, walk." Perhaps the reason Peter had no money is that he had already shared it with the other believers. But he had something so much better to offer—the healing power of the living Christ, present in these two apostles. He offered the man dignity, starting with that first directive, "Look at us!" He offered the miraculous touch of the Master, a touch that restored the man's body to wholeness and his life to relationships and community. The man didn't start by crawling or slowly shuffling; he jumped to his feet, walked and jumped and praised God, creating quite a commotion! The whole event caused wonder and amazement among the people. The presence of God was revealed in their midst.

We can imagine that this man went on to join the fellowship of believers and enjoy his share of the food and all the benefits of belonging, including offering his own time and energy to bless the others. How much better an outcome than the coins he originally wanted!

From the earliest days of the Church, one expression of faith in Jesus and wholehearted participation in his community has been generosity. Compassion for the poor, acts of mercy, and financial gifts have always been hallmarks of Jesus' followers. Practical assistance to relieve human suffering and meet people's most basic needs comes right from the heart of God.

Later in the story of the Early Church, a famine overtook one region, so believers from other places sent emergency food aid. For us, 2,000 years later in a globalized world, the opportunity to use our finances to help is taken to a whole new level. Now we're not just aware of regional needs, but are exposed to economic disasters, war, terrorism, and the suffering of refugees on a global scale. In addition, as believers, we are presented with unprecedented opportunities to use financial resources to assist and empower the emerging church around the world. Silver and gold? We have some, but …

Is money our most valuable resource? We might be tempted to believe that it is, and some of our brothers and sisters living in contexts of poverty might also believe, like the lame beggar, that the best thing we could offer them would be money. And yet, how far would our pooled resources go, in the face of global poverty and the unprecedented opportunities for expanding the church? If our money is all we have, or the most important thing we have, we are in trouble.

Some international partners in contexts of poverty might believe, like the lame man believed, that the best thing we could offer them would be money. Could they be right? Under what conditions?

> **What do you have to share with others that is more valuable than money?**
>
> **Do you share it?**

In most places where the church is growing exponentially, it is doing so without huge infusions of foreign money. In some of the countries where the gospel is spreading like wildfire, believers must meet secretly to avoid detection by governmental or religious authorities who are hostile to the gospel. Christians meet in homes, like they did in the Second Chapter of Acts. Most groups are led by laypeople, often women.

Even in countries where it is legal and safe for the faithful to gather, some of the most fruitful models of church planting are simple and inexpensive. Community Church Planting (CCP), also known as Village Church Planting (VCP), is a model capable of exponential growth based on several key biblical principles. One of these is, "The resources are in the harvest." That is, as we lead people to faith in Christ and make disciples, God will provide people to extend the work, and the new believers will use their own lives and material resources to fuel the movement. The people's homes, food, affection, care for one another, practical service to one another, prayers, practical gifts and spiritual gifts will be a far greater asset than monetary currency, either local or foreign. Just like in Acts 2, when the Spirit comes on people, they experience radical generosity as they share their lives with one another in community.

> **Do you believe that "the resources are in the harvest?"**
> **Does your local church believe that seeing new people come to faith and join the church will be part of God's provision for future leaders in the church, servants for ministries in the church, and financial support?**

Is there a role for us as outsiders? We want our partnerships with the family of God in its many expressions around the world to be healthy, not perpetuating alien, expensive models of church or fostering a dependency mindset. The primary factor in healthy partnerships is the quality of the relationships. One of the great benefits of belonging to a denomination is that we are truly connectional; our leaders walk alongside Free Methodist leaders in many nations, in friendship and mutual respect and love. Not every donor needs to know every beneficiary personally; our networks are trustworthy and are built on relationships. Mission leaders and church leaders plan together for strategic sharing of resources, including but not limited to finances.

Is there a role for us as outsiders? Do you think there is, and if so, what is it?

There certainly are times and situations when dollars can be leveraged for great good. When expectations are clear and the purpose and timeline for support are understood, we can invest well. From preschool through university and seminary degrees, education builds capacity in people and leads to self-sufficiency. Supporting mercy ministries like care of vulnerable children, widows, and people in need of medical assistance can put resources into the hands of those most able to serve in these ways. Funding national leaders and cross-cultural missionaries so they can devote their best energies to the spread of the gospel often makes sense. Working with people to provide sustainable livelihoods, agricultural improvements, and other practical development projects is another way of helping them to become capable helpers of others. Many forms of resource sharing can be used by God to do on a macro scale what the earliest believers did on the micro scale in their community.

Silver and gold? We have some. But the presence and power of Jesus will always be the greatest asset we could ever offer to anyone in need. Coins in a cup are limited and short-term; walking and jumping and praising God are so much better!

Do the needs of the world weigh heavily on you? Do you experience a lot of guilt that you can't do more? Why or why not?

Under what conditions do you believe it is healthy for the non-poor in countries like ours to make financial commitments to fund Christian work in parts of the world where people live in poverty?

What cautions should we have about the impact of our generosity? Is it our responsibility to partner only in healthy ways, or should we just share what we have and leave the results up to God?

Questions for Further Reflection:

1. Have you ever "tasted an appetizer" of the kind of community described in Acts 2:42-47? Tell us about it.

2. If your church started a practice where people sold possessions and shared them with the poor members of the church, what concerns would you have?

3. How much do you think the community around your church building knows about your church? If they know you're there, does anything about your church appeal to them?

4. Some international partners in contexts of poverty might believe, like the lame man believed, that the best thing we could offer them would be money. Could they be right? Under what conditions?

5. What do you have to share with others that is more valuable than money? Do you share it?

6. Do the needs of the world weigh heavily on you? Do you experience a lot of guilt that you can't do more? Why or why not?

7. Is there a role for us as outsiders? Do you think there is, and if so, what is it?

8. Do you believe that "the resources are in the harvest?" Does your local church believe that seeing new people come to faith and join the church will be part of God's provision for future leaders in the church, servants for ministries in the church, and financial support?

9. Under what conditions do you believe it is healthy for the non-poor in countries like ours to make financial commitments to fund Christian work in parts of the world where people live in poverty?

10. What cautions should we have about the impact of our generosity? Is it our responsibility to partner only in healthy ways, or should we just share what we have and leave the results up to God?

THE BULLSEYE ON GOD'S TARGET

When Jesus was 30 years old and just beginning his public ministry, he went to the synagogue at his hometown of Nazareth and was given the scroll of Isaiah to read. He opened it up to Isaiah 61:1 and began to read, "The Spirit of the Lord God is upon me, because he has anointed me to proclaim good news to the poor; proclaim liberty to the captives and recovering of sight to the blind, to set at liberty those who are oppressed, to proclaim the year of the Lord's favor." (Luke 4:18-19) He went on to declare, "Today this Scripture has been fulfilled in your hearing." (Luke 4:22)

Some have called this passage Jesus' "Kingdom Manifesto." By reading from Isaiah 61 and then claiming to be the fulfillment of that Old Testament prophesy, he connected his identity and the work he was about to begin with all that God had done down through the history of his people and all that was prophesied for the future.

What does the word Manifesto mean to you?

Jesus came to demonstrate God's passion and live out God's priorities in front of his own people and the watching world. Where were his priorities? Who were the recipients of his passion?

The poor. The captives. The blind. The oppressed. These are the recipients of his good news and the beneficiaries of his liberating and healing acts. He proclaimed God's favor on these—the last, the least, and the left behind. No wonder some have called this the "Upside Down Kingdom."

> **What evidence can you think of in the gospels that Jesus actually lived out the priorities he identified here?**
>
> **Recall a moment when you felt marginalized or on the outside, looking in. What did you most yearn for in that situation?**

If we continue reading Isaiah 61 where Jesus left off, we might see some more surprises. After proclaiming the year of the Lord's favor, the prophet continues, "and the day of vengeance of our God; to comfort all who mourn … that they may be called oaks of righteousness, the planting of the Lord that he may be glorified." (Isaiah 61:2b, 4b) Our God not only declares his favor and blessing on these troubled ones (the poor, the captives, the blind, the oppressed); he also executes vengeance against the wicked and comforts those who mourn.

These people know mourning. Life has not gone well. They may feel God-forsaken and worthless. They probably have internalized the negative message that society and their own misfortunes have drilled into their heads and hearts: They are losers. Others are the powerful; they are the powerless. Others get ahead; they fall behind. They may believe the religious lie that they are cursed by God. They may believe the lie of Satan that they are unloved and unlovable. They likely believe that their lives will account for nothing.

> **How do those of us who have, for the most part, benefited from structures of power and affluence gain a sensitivity to the plight of those who are poor and powerless?**
>
> **When people around us have internalized negative and hopeless messages about themselves and their lives, what can we do to help them rewrite that script?**

> **How has our culture blinded us by promoting values that don't reflect what we read in Isaiah 61 and see in the ministry of Jesus?**

But look at what this pathetic-sounding group will become when they receive the good news and all its benefits: oaks of righteousness! They will stand tall, put down roots, and reach up with towering branches; they will produce leaves and acorns and multiply into more strong, sturdy, life-giving trees. The Lord has planted them, and they will glorify him.

When I travel to countries where the gospel has taken root and grown into a mighty forest, I often think of this passage. When missionary John Wesley Haley followed God's call to enter Burundi, could he ever have imagined that the church he planted would one day boast far more members than the church "back home" in Canada and the United States?

Several of our largest and most fruitful mission fields in the world were initially begun or nurtured in their earliest years by single female missionaries, laboring with very little financial support and almost no expectation of making it back to their sending countries alive. To some in their day, they might have been viewed as the weaker sex, second-class ambassadors, but the tremendous fruitfulness of the churches they planted sets the record straight.

Many of our global partners live and work in places of great poverty and inexhaustible human need. Most are poor and work among the poor. When Bishop Elie Buconyori of Burundi was alive, I asked him about the average per capita income of Burundi. He answered, "Well, it's $2 U.S. a day in the country as a whole, but we Free Methodists work with the *poor* people!"

What do we believe about the innate and developed capacities of our loved ones in contexts of poverty? Can we learn to see them as our equals, colleagues who far surpass us in understanding their own culture and often have insights into the Word of God that would enlighten us if we could listen? What have they discovered by hammering out theology in the crucible of cultures that resemble the Old Testament context far more than ours does? Do we bother to investigate their worldview?

I'm afraid that many times we exclusively live by our own cultural assumptions and violate the values of our friends. My "kindergarten" lesson in this reality came when an African family joined the church I pastored in Rochester, New York. I sent 15-year-old Alex on an errand to the corner store to buy about $13 worth of food, so I gave him a $20 bill. When he returned, I asked him for the change. He looked at me like I had wounded him. Eyes locked on mine, he reluctantly reached into his pocket and gave me the $7. I was a little miffed, thinking he had attempted to get one over on me by not returning my change. Then I read a book called _African Friends and Money Matters_. One of the first contrasts between how Africans view money and how Westerners view it is, "To whom does change belong?" The author said that in Africa, if you send someone on an errand, the change is their tip. So rather than Alex ripping me off, I was shortchanging him! He thought he had earned a $7 windfall, but I took it away. How much I had to learn. That book taught me literally 98 other contrasts, most of them a complete surprise. My "right" way is not the only way; I must become a student of others' ways of understanding.

> *Have you experienced a cross-cultural blooper like this one? What cultural misunderstandings were involved in your personal experience?*

Returning to Isaiah's prophecy, the next verse brings the Great Reversal to another level: "They shall build up the ancient ruins; they shall raise up the former devastations; they shall repair the ruined cities, the devastations of many generations." (Isaiah 61:4) Who are the powerful redemptive actors in this prophecy? Whose initiative and cooperation with God will build up ancient ruins, raise up former devastations, and repair ruined cities? The recipients of the good news: the poor, the captives, the blind, and the oppressed. "*They*" will do it! God's saving work in these people's lives transforms them into agents of God's *shalom*, bringing peace and wholeness to the world, restoring what has been broken.

> *Isaiah 61:4 paints a picture of wide-ranging works of restoration and shalom, accomplished by those whose lives have been transformed by the good news. How big is your imagination when it comes to the expected results of your own salvation?*

Might they still be poor? Probably. Might they live in captivity to unjust economic systems? No doubt. Might their eyes still not see in the physical realm? Perhaps. Might they operate under oppressive regimes? Often.

And yet, they are oaks of righteousness, the planting of the Lord, and they bring glory to him. They exude life and fecundity; they herald the kingdom of God and work for all its manifestations in human life and society.

Seeds that were once planted in the mission fields of the world have in many places grown to produce vast forests with countless trees. The nature of the gospel is that it contains within it the potential to multiply exponentially. We live at an opportune moment in human history, when we can join forces with the global Church to transform whole societies and bless the entire creation, for the glory of God.

> *What life-changing good news have you received? How has it changed your life?*
>
> *Have you been under the impression that the Christian faith around the world is on the rise or on the decline? What could you do to test your opinion?*

Questions for Further Reflection:

1. Recall a moment when you felt marginalized or on the outside, looking in. What did you most yearn for in that situation?

2. What does the word manifesto mean to you?

3. What evidence can you think of in the gospels that Jesus actually lived out the priorities he identified here?

4. Have you experienced a cross-cultural blooper like the one the author describes when she sent the African boy on an errand? What cultural misunderstandings were involved in your personal experience?

5. How do those of us who have, for the most part, benefited from structures of power and affluence, gain a sensitivity to the plight of those who are poor and powerless?

6. When people around us have internalized negative and hopeless messages about themselves and their lives, what can we do to help them rewrite that script?

7. How has our culture blinded us by promoting values that don't reflect what we read in Isaiah 61 and see in the ministry of Jesus?

8. Isaiah 61:4 paints a picture of wide-ranging works of restoration and shalom, accomplished by those whose lives have been transformed by the good news. How big is your imagination when it comes to the expected results of your own salvation?

9. What life-changing good news have you received? How has it changed your life?

10. Have you been under the impression that the Christian faith around the world is on the rise or on the decline? What could you do to test your opinion?

SUSTAINING SONGS FOR THE OVERSTUFFED

We often speak of partnering with the global church as a two-way street, a mutually-beneficial arrangement. Sometimes I wonder whether people think we're telling the truth about that. Doesn't a lot of money flow from the American partner to the partner in the developing world? What flows the other direction that could possibly be as valuable?

International Child Care Ministries (ICCM) has recently created a form of partnership called "Connected Communities." Several churches in the United States have now chosen to embark on a long-term relationship with Free Methodist leaders in another country for the good of the children, church, and community in that place—but also for some important benefits to the US partner.

One pair of Connected Communities is Pearce Memorial Free Methodist Church in Rochester, NY, and the Free Methodist Church and School in Nzige, Rwanda. Pearce members and the pastor tell how their own spiritual lives and their community of faith have been enriched. Pastor Wally Fleming says, "The people of Nzige have become our teachers."

How did Wally get to know and love this remote community in rural Rwanda? First, he and a few others made an exploratory trip with the goal of simply listening. Pearce people wanted to know the people in the Nzige Church, to hear the story of their community and learn about how God had entered their story and transformed their lives.

How did this church begin? How did the Holy Spirit work to draw lost people into the Kingdom of God? Why did they start a preschool? What vision caused them to haul rocks from the riverbed and make bricks with their own hands to build the first classrooms?

Were you surprised that a mission team would go all the way to Africa for the first time with the main agenda of simply listening? Could it have been worth the money and time invested? Why or why not?

The parents at Nzige, Rwanda, had hauled rocks from the riverbank and made bricks with their own hands to build the preschool. What do you think about their commitment to educate the children of their community? Can you think of similar stories of commitment and sacrifice here?

Rwandan leaders were also eager to learn about Pearce. What is the church like? How do these people worship God and serve their community? What missionaries from the history of the Free Methodist Church in Rwanda are known to these Americans? Why would Pearce send a delegation across the ocean to Rwanda to explore a partnership?

Stories were heard and valued, and a relationship was formed. Over the next couple of years, at the invitation of leaders in Rwanda, visiting teams from Pearce conducted workshops on teaching methods for young children and children with special needs and pastors' continuing education seminars. Nzige's leaders identified other practical goals—a water storage tank, land for gardening, chickens so the school children could eat eggs, and playground equipment. ICCM's leader in Rwanda sent photos to Pearce so the church could delight in what they had envisioned and provided together.
Projecting pictures on the screen at Pearce brought laughter and joy: children holding armloads of live chickens, 3-year-olds trying to peel hard boiled eggs, and the very first giddy riders on the new swing set—teachers!

What principles for healthy partnerships do you see in the Pearce-Nzige pairing?

Rwandan ICCM National Coordinator Ephaste Niyigena describes how Pearce's investment in the children's lives has brought a new awareness to these parents that their children are valuable and full of great potential. He continues, "Pearce people have agreed to share with the people of Nzige love and money." Note the order. What have the Nzige people shared with Pearce?

One term for the "non-poor" in Development literature is the "salaried and caloried." That phrase reminds me of a scene from A. A. Milne's *Winnie the Pooh*. Pooh, a stuffed bear, goes into his friend Rabbit's home through a hole and eats and eats. In fact, he eats so much that when he tries to go out the same rabbit hole, he's too fat to squeeze through! His head is out but his backside is in. Winnie the Pooh is just going to have to stay stuck until he loses enough weight to budge through the opening. He gets discouraged, but his friends on the outside gather around him and, in Milne's version, read him "sustaining stories." In Disney's version, his friends sing him "sustaining songs."

Jesus said some things that make me think of this image. In Matthew 18:3 he said, "Truly I say to you, unless you turn and become like children, you will never enter the kingdom of heaven." To get into his kingdom, we adults must somehow get smaller and younger. In the next verse, Jesus clarifies that he is talking about humility: "Whoever humbles himself like this child is the greatest in the kingdom of heaven."

> **How do you understand Jesus' claim that to enter his kingdom we must be more childlike, and the greatest of all is the humble person?**

For us, the "salaried and caloried," living out the Christian faith can be an uphill battle with pride. Deep inside, we believe that we deserve our wealth; it is a sign of God's blessing and favor; and it is truly ours. We may learn that we are not actually owners, but stewards of our possessions, but it is very hard for us to believe that. We have many material and societal advantages, including access to education and opportunities that enhance our ability to improve our economic condition. We are privileged, and somehow can't see that if we flip the logic of our preconceptions around, we are saying some terrible things that are not true. For instance, should our Christian brothers and sisters who live in extreme poverty and under unjust governments, with entrenched economic systems stacked against them believe that they are *not* blessed and favored by God? That he doesn't care for them, or at least that he cares more for us? We need help.

Jesus said another puzzling thing: "It is easier for a camel to go through the eye of a needle than for someone who is rich to enter the kingdom of God" (Matthew 19:24). Some scholars claim that the needle's eye was a small gate in the wall of Jerusalem; others say the Greek word for "camel" is almost like the word for a sailor's heavy rope. So, take your pick: picture the ridiculous sight of a real camel trying to get even his nose through the eye of a sewing needle, a wild hyperbole. Or, picture a camel getting down on his belly and squeezing through a small opening in a stone wall. Or, picture trying to thread the largest rope you've ever seen through the tiny eye of a normal needle. In any case, Jesus' point is clear: It's hard, if not impossible. We're stuck in the rabbit hole.

> *How do you understand Jesus' words that it's harder for a camel to go through the eye of a needle than for a rich person to enter the kingdom of God?*
>
> *How do you define "rich"?*
>
> *What evidence of excess do you see in our culture?*

Thankfully, God has provided some members of our global family to sing us sustaining songs while we find a way to get smaller. Honest friendships shatter stereotypes and help us to see beyond categories of race, nationality, and status. We get to truly know people who are created in the image of God and endowed with rights and gifts like we are. They, too, are fallen sinners who have been found by the grace of God and are on the journey toward wholeness. Being stuck in that rabbit hole can give us time to listen—to figure out that our own stories have created some blind spots in us, and to discover that the singers who sustain us have gained a lot of wisdom in their lives. For instance, since the 1994 genocide that tore apart the country of Rwanda, our partners there have learned hard lessons on repentance, forgiveness and reconciliation; they can become our teachers. If we will be still and listen, we'll realize that God was active in their world long before our stories converged with each other's—and he is active in our current predicament, too. After all, who sends friends whose songs help us to embrace humility? Maybe we'll shed a few pounds of excess stuff or divest ourselves of our presumption of superiority, and slip right through that rabbit hole.

> *How do you like the image of Winnie the Pooh stuck in the rabbit hole? How does it speak to you?*
>
> *Has anyone sustained you with stories or songs that have opened your eyes to your own blind spots and helped you to humble yourself?*

Given enough time to build trust, cross-cultural relationships can expand the worldview and open the eyes of people on both sides. We can all learn that accumulation and worldly success are not the aim in life; the abundant life that Jesus promises is more about love, justice, and peace. We stand to bless and be blessed by sharing life across boundaries and oceans. The winding road called "Partnership" is definitely a two-way street.

Questions for Further Reflection:

1. Were you surprised that a mission team would go all the way to Africa for the first time with the main agenda of simply listening? Could it have been worth the money and time invested? Why or why not?

2. The parents at Nzige, Rwanda, had hauled rocks from the riverbank and made bricks with their own hands to build the preschool. What do you think about their commitment to educate the children of their community? Can you think of similar stories of commitment and sacrifice here?

3. What principles for healthy partnerships do you see in the Pearce-Nzige pairing?

4. How do you understand Jesus' claim that to enter his kingdom we must be more childlike, and the greatest of all is the humble person?

5. How do you understand Jesus' words that it's harder for a camel to go through the eye of a needle than for a rich person to enter the kingdom of God?

6. How do you define "rich"?

7. What evidence of excess do you see in our culture?

8. How do you like the image of Winnie the Pooh stuck in the rabbit hole? How does it speak to you?

9. Has anyone sustained you with stories or songs that have opened your eyes to your own blind spots and helped you to humble yourself?

10. What opportunities for cross-cultural relationships that go deep enough to change us for the better can you think of, for those of us who do not leave our country?

SECTION III

REACHING CROSS CULTURALLY
IN THE UNITED STATES
- Gerald Coates

START SIMPLY: MAKING FRIENDS WITH FIRST GENERATION IMMIGRANTS

Ya Feng stood weeping. My wife, Jan, had just shared the news we were moving to another city. We had reached out to the immigrants in our city for the past seven years, and Ya Feng was a friend. Jan taught her children piano lessons. We enjoyed special occasions together. Ours was the first American home she had been in, though she had lived over 10 years in our city. No American had ever invited her to their home. Now that relationship was being severed. In broken sobs and through her husband's translation the pain came out, "Before you came, I didn't have any friends."

How friendly are you to first generation immigrants? How many friends do you have that are first generation immigrants? How many generations has your family resided in the United States?

"Permanent relationships are what Americans fear the most. This is a nation whose most fundamental social relationship is the casual acquaintance."[1] One of the primary needs of those who have come to live with us from other countries is significant relationships. Imagine what it is like to leave behind your network of relatives and friendships to venture into a new country.

---

1 Faul, Stephanie, *Xenophobe's Guide to the Americans*, Oval Books, 1994, 1.

What are the things that make you uncomfortable about talking with people from other countries?

It is interesting that Abraham, sometimes referred to as the father of our faith, was in a similar situation. God's first words to Abram were to call him to be an immigrant: "Go from your country, your people and your father's household to the land I will show you." (Genesis 12:1) The promise was that he would be made into a great nation, but the road to the promise was treacherous and risky. He had to leave behind his security and travel to an unknown destination. When he reached Canaan it was a land in the midst of famine. So Abram went to live in Egypt for a while. Abram had already left his home land and was a foreigner in Canaan. Now, he was a foreigner in Egypt. As he was entering Egypt he convinced his wife Sarai to pose as his sister, rather than his wife. From our perspective we can hardly understand Abraham's disregard for the sanctity of their marriage. But it is a vivid picture of how fear can be the motivating factor for a foreigner. Abram wants to be accepted in the new culture.

Describe a situation in which you were in the minority and how it made you feel. What could someone have done to make you feel welcomed and valued?

It is a challenge for most of us living in our birth culture to bridge the gap and understand what it is like for someone to live with us from another culture. "After all, they came here—they should learn our language and our ways." It is amazing how few Americans take a similar approach when visiting another culture.

How would you describe your general attitude toward the first generation immigrants living among us?

Let's push back into our spiritual heritage and realize our roots are in being strangers. The first call to Abram is to be an immigrant. Historically, our primary identification is not with the Canaanites or the Egyptians but with the immigrant Abraham. Moses instructed the Israelites that when they finally settled into the promised land, when they had gathered the first fruits from the soil of the land, place them in a basket and take it to the priests and declare before the Lord, "My father was a wandering Aramean, and he went down into Egypt with a few people and lived there and became a great nation, powerful and numerous. But the Egyptians mistreated us and made us suffer, subjecting us to harsh labor." (Deuteronomy 26:5-6) We have interests in reaching those from other cultures who live among us. First, we believe Christ died for all and the gospel has no national boundaries. There is not a preferred culture in the kingdom of God. The globalization taking place is a huge opportunity for the expansion of the kingdom.

> **What would you identify as the major thing that inhibits you from reaching out to first generation immigrants? What might you do to be able to overcome that inhibition?**

Second, the best people to reach people from other cultures are people who are bi-cultural. It is strategic to be reaching out to those from other cultures, because they have a more effective reach back into their native culture as well as across cultural lines here.[2]

Reaching those from other cultures starts with building relationships. It's not rocket science. Almost anyone can do it. All it takes is an open heart. When we started reaching to those who are first generation immigrants we began by visiting Chinese restaurants during off peak times. It was as simple as having conversations and showing interest without being nosey and pushy. We noticed that in the summer, some of the restaurant owners' children were spending most of the day in the restaurant. At first, we simply took coloring books and crayons for them. Eventually, after a long time of relationship building, we asked permission to take the kids to the park.

---

2 See Boyd, David, *You Don't Have to Cross the Ocean to Reach the World: The Power of Local Cross-Cultural Ministry.*

What are some activities you can participate in with people who don't share a common language?

First generation immigrants can use a lot of assistance. They just need someone they can trust. Imagine what it would be like for you to go to a country where you don't know the language and cultural norms and try to get a driver's license. Imagine trying to purchase a home and getting the utilities hooked up. Imagine trying to find a doctor and being unable to describe what is wrong. Imagine what it is like to try to establish a business. Imagine trying to learn the language when you work from 9 a.m. to 9 p.m. 364 days a year. Undoubtedly, there are many means for assistance in the United States for immigrants, but one need our government can't provide is a friend to trust.

What might you do to improve your own network of friends to reflect the diversity of your city?

I remember one morning in Kaohsiung, Taiwan, when I was to meet a driver who was to take our family to a gathering of pastors where I was to teach. The drive was to take more than an hour. I had no instructions but where I was to meet the driver. We met at the specified location at the exact time. He smiled and welcomed us, but we soon learned we had no language in common. The fact he had breakfast in the car for us was comforting; otherwise we might have thought we had been picked up by a complete stranger. Since we had no idea of where we were going or exactly how long it would take, we were at the mercy of the driver. We smiled at each other, but that was the extent of our interaction. He was playing some music on the radio. I couldn't understand a word of it. I didn't even know which of three possible languages it might be in. All of a sudden I heard, "Hallelujah" in the lyrics. I turned to the driver and said, "Hallelujah!" He smiled and responded, "Hallelujah." I then said, "Amen!" and he did, too! We had two words in common.

What are things you share in common with people of all cultures?

I'll admit that was an uncomfortable situation, but it is one I highly value. I have some small inkling of what those who are immigrating here must feel—alone and dependent on others.

The Lord may never call you to go to another country to preach or teach, but he is bringing people from all over the world to our cities and towns. We can be the first point of friendship to those who don't even yet know they need Jesus. It just makes sense. After all, I'm just a fifth generation immigrant myself.

Use your phone or other device to look up usa.com. Find your state and city and click on the population tab. Look at the diversity of the population for your city. How many friends do you have from people groups other than your own?

Questions for Further Reflection:

1. How friendly are you to first generation immigrants? How many friends do you have that are first generation immigrants? How many generations has your family resided in the United States?

2. What are the things that make you uncomfortable about talking with people from other countries?

3. Describe a situation in which you were in the minority and how it made you feel. What could someone have done to make you feel welcomed and valued?

4. How would you describe your general attitude toward the first generation immigrants living among us?

5. What would you identify as the major thing that inhibits you from reaching out to first generation immigrants?

6. What might you do to be able to overcome that inhibition?

7. What are some activities you can participate with people who don't share a common language?

8. What might you do to improve your own network of friends to reflect the diversity of your city?

9. What are things you share in common with people of all cultures?

10. Use your phone or other device to look up usa.com. Find your state and city and click on the population tab. Look at the diversity of the population for your city. How many friends do you have from people groups other than your own?

EXTEND NATURALLY: ENGAGING THE PEOPLE WE ENCOUNTER

My friend, Dr. Linda Adams, who wrote Chapters 5-8 in this book, tells the story of her experience welcoming central African Free Methodists to their church in Rochester, New York:

> On a normal Sunday morning in May 2007, seven members of a family from the Democratic Republic of the Congo made a pretty grand entrance into the sanctuary of New Hope Free Methodist Church in Rochester, NY and changed our church. With 28-year-old Heritage interpreting, the father Prudence said to me, "We are orphans. We have no mother, no father; no motherland, no fatherland. The Free Methodist Church is our family, and you are our mother!" A little taken aback, I blurted out, "Welcome home!"
>
> We had so much to learn from this family of 11 and the 22 others from Burundi who joined us later that year. Their prayers and strong faith, their family solidarity and eagerness to learn English and fit in with our church family were a joy for us to discover. In time, we also heard their stories of extreme suffering, of tribal conflict, child soldiering, banishment from their homeland, and a massacre in a refugee camp that killed their 7-year-old daughter in front of their eyes. We also found out that we had more to offer than we had ever dreamed—appliances and household necessities, English lessons and driving lessons, orientation to our grocery stores and the maze of social services available to refugees, but most of all, friendship and love. The day our African brothers and sisters found their "long lost family," we were radically changed for the better. We thank God for that day in May.

> **What do you think are the best ways to welcome a person from another culture? If you were in Dr. Adams place, how might you have responded differently?**

In Dr. Adam's story there was a crucial moment. When presented with the opportunity to welcome the first generation immigrant, she could have shrunk back thinking of all the inconveniences this would mean for her congregation, or she could simply say, "Welcome home!" That moment in time was a reflection of her theology. A sound biblical theology.

Notice in succession from Exodus, Leviticus and Deuteronomy God's special instruction for how the Israelites are to treat the foreigner:

> *Do not oppress a foreigner; you yourselves know how it feels to be foreigners, because you were foreigners in Egypt. Exodus 23:9*

> *'When a foreigner resides among you in your land, do not mistreat them. The foreigner residing among you must be treated as your native-born. Love them as yourself, for you were foreigners in Egypt. I am the Lord your God.' (Leviticus 19:33-34)*

> *For the Lord your God is God of gods and Lord of lords, the great God, mighty and awesome, who shows no partiality and accepts no bribes. He defends the cause of the fatherless and the widow, and loves the foreigner residing among you, giving them food and clothing. And you are to love those who are foreigners, for you yourselves were foreigners in Egypt. (Deuteronomy 10:17-19)*

> **Who are the foreigners in your community you are most likely to encounter?**

Notice the instructions: do not oppress them, do not mistreat them; and love them (as yourself). Notice the substantiation for the instructions — it is repeated three times, "you were foreigners in Egypt."

> **What cross cultural experiences have you had that inform you on how someone who is new to our culture might feel?**

Among those receiving this command in Deuteronomy, only two people would have been adults in Egypt. Joshua and Caleb. Many of the people would not have any active memory of being slaves in Egypt. All they knew were the stories of their parents and grandparents. Most of these receiving the instruction would have been born in the 40 years of wandering in the wilderness. But the instructions talk about the collective understanding of what it means to be a foreigner. They all had that in common. Not a person in the whole of Israel would have been at home in the land they were going. They were all foreigners, and that was to inform them as to how they were to treat foreigners.

But there is another level of substantiation for the instructions. "God loves the foreigner residing among you … and you are to love those who are foreigners."

> **Have you experienced any place to be more open to outsiders than others? What are these places, and what aspects of them make them more open to outsiders?**

That's a biblical perspective that informs how we respond to the foreigners living among us. The first level is to not oppress them. The second level is to treat them as if they are native born. The third level is to love them as we love ourselves. The fourth level is to love them as God loves them. Dr. Adams' reception of the family from the Democratic Republic of the Congo was a level four response. "Welcome home!" It is what God does. He welcomes the stranger. Even Jesus used this as an understanding of what it means to welcome him. *"I was hungry and you gave me something to eat, I was thirsty and you gave me something to drink, I was a stranger and you invited me in, I needed clothes and you clothed me, I was sick and you looked after me, I was in prison and you came to visit me.'* (Matthew 25:35-36) The word translated "stranger" is the Greek word *xenos,* which is also translated "foreigner."

> **What have you learned about your culture from an outsider that was interesting or curious to you?**

It is the same word used by Paul to describe those of us who were Gentiles by birth.

> Therefore, remember that formerly you who are Gentiles by birth and called "uncircumcised" by those who call themselves "the circumcision" (which is done in the body by human hands)— remember that at that time you were separate from Christ, excluded from citizenship in Israel and foreigners to the covenants of the promise, without hope and without God in the world. But now in Christ Jesus you who once were far away have been brought near by the blood of Christ. -Ephesians 2:11-13

What God did for us is to include us in his promise that was originally made through the nation of Israel. But even this is the mystery of the gospel. Paul describes it to the church at Colossae:

> I have become its (the church's) servant by the commission God gave me to present to you the word of God in its fullness— the mystery that has been kept hidden for ages and generations, but is now disclosed to the Lord's people. To them God has chosen to make known among the Gentiles the glorious riches of this mystery, which is Christ in you, the hope of glory. -Colossians 1:25-27

> **What could you do differently to make it more likely to encounter people of another culture on a regular basis?**

God's heart is for those who are foreigners to Him. Jesus came to seek and save those who were lost. God sends the rain on the just and the unjust. We are in no place to regard ourselves from a position of prestige or power or privilege. Our identification is as foreigners whom God loves and we, in turn, welcome those whom God loves.

> **What is your response to the idea of being a foreigner accepted by God through Jesus Christ?**

We live in a day in which we encounter people for whom this country was not their country of birth. Our response to them reflects our theology. At one level it is good if we are not oppressing them or cheating them. Unfortunately, there are plenty of people taking advantage of first generation immigrants. But what would happen if the church of Jesus Christ in the United States was known for its adherence to the theological framework which treats the foreigner as the native-born and loves them with a welcoming love?

> **As you have observed others interacting cross culturally, what have you learned to imitate? What you have learned to avoid?**

When our children were small we taught them the concept of moral minimums and moral excellence. We would often frame it in terms of good, better and best. As an example, we would train them that when a guest came into our home, the moral minimum was to stand up when they came into the room and say "hello." But it would be better for them to go over and to shake their hand and say something like, "It's good to meet you!" But it would be best if they would look them in the eye, shake their hand, and ask them about their trip and engage in conversation about what is important in their lives.

It terms of engaging in cross cultural ministry, there is the moral minimum of not oppressing the foreigner; there is the better option of treating them as if they were natural-born citizens; and there is the best option of welcoming them into relationship fueled by God's love for them.

> **What is your plan for this coming week to engage with someone who is culturally different from you?**

Questions for Further Reflection:

1. What do you think are the best ways to welcome a person from another culture?

2. If you were in Dr. Adams' place, how might you have responded differently?

3. Who are the foreigners in your community you are most likely to encounter?

4. What cross-cultural experiences have you had that inform you on how someone who is new to our culture might feel?

5. Have you experienced any place to be more open to outsiders than others? What are these places, and what aspects of them make them more open to outsiders?

6. What have you learned about your culture from an outsider that was interesting or curious to you?

7. What could you do differently to make it more likely to encounter people of another culture on a regular basis?

8. What is your response to the idea of being a foreigner accepted by God through Jesus Christ?

9. As you have observed others interacting cross culturally, what have you learned to imitate? What you have learned to avoid?

10. What is your plan for this coming week to engage with someone who is culturally different from you?

INCREASE INTERNALLY: GOING BEYOND THE EXPECTED

In 2013 I had the opportunity to visit the home of Corrie ten Boom. It was a mysterious place to be realizing the deep hatred that had forced the ten Boom family to provide this refuge for Jews trying to escape the horrors of the Holocaust. I was standing in the home of a family that lost their home, business, and their lives for the love of others.

What trends can you see over time that perpetuate hatred for a certain nationality?

Corrie ten Boom shared about her experience following a presentation she made in Munich after the war.

> It was at a church service in Munich that I saw him, a former S.S. man who had stood guard at the shower room door in the processing center at Ravensbruck. He was the first of our actual jailers that I had seen since that time. And suddenly it was all there – the roomful of mocking men, the heaps of clothing, Betsie's pain-blanched face.
>
> He came up to me as the church was emptying, beaming and bowing. "How grateful I am for your message, Fraulein," he said. "To think that, as you say, He has washed my sins away!" His hand was thrust out to shake mine. And I, who had preached so often to the people in Bloemendaal the need to forgive, kept my hand at my side.

Even as the angry, vengeful thoughts boiled through me, I saw the sin of them. Jesus Christ had died for this man; was I going to ask for more? Lord Jesus, I prayed, forgive me and help me to forgive him. I tried to smile, I struggled to raise my hand. I could not. I felt nothing, not the slightest spark of warmth or charity. And so again I breathed a silent prayer. Jesus, I prayed, I cannot forgive him. Give me Your forgiveness.

As I took his hand the most incredible thing happened. From my shoulder along my arm and through my hand a current seemed to pass from me to him, while into my heart sprang a love for this stranger that almost overwhelmed me. And so I discovered that it is not on our forgiveness any more than on our goodness that the world's healing hinges, but on His. When He tells us to love our enemies, He gives, along with the command, the love itself.

Who are the people you find most difficult to love? Why?

The intense hatred lived out in World War II had its birth in extreme nationalism. It is not the only example of xenophobia fueling cruelty. We have experienced this in our own country at many different levels, from the lynching of African Americans to the imprisonment of anti-war sympathizers in World War I.

But there is something transforming about the love of God in Jesus Christ that transcends the normal fear-based reactions. Even in the Old Testament there are these hidden gems of God's amazing love.

Identify any current cultural trends that might run contrary to the command to love our enemy.

You might remember the story of Naaman. He was commander of the army of the king of Aram. Aram was the country northeast of Israel, and was situated in the place of modern-day Syria. We remember the story because Naaman went to Elisha for healing from his leprosy. It's an odd story because Naaman almost misses his opportunity for healing because he doesn't like Elisha's prescription for dipping seven times in the Jordan River. But at the insistence of his servant, he concedes and is healed. Not only is he healed, he becomes a believer in God.

The part of the story that we often overlook is in the introduction.

> Now bands of raiders from Aram had gone out and had taken captive a young girl from Israel, and she served Naaman's wife. She said to her mistress, "If only my master would see the prophet who is in Samaria! He would cure him of his leprosy." -2 Kings 5:2-3

What do you think God might do in your life to break down any long-seated hatred toward another people group?

A young girl is the behind-the-scenes hero of the story. She has been taken captive and forced into slavery. From her position of slavery she has compassion on Naaman. I can't say that if I were in the same situation I would have had compassion on my captor.

One of the things that keeps us from loving the foreigner among us is deeply rooted in our national and personal psyche. It may be that our nationalism trumps our compassion. It may be that personal hurt transcends our love of our neighbors. Whatever the case, if these deep-seated emotions are a hindrance to the gospel of Jesus, they must be overcome.

What could you or your small group do to create an atmosphere of love and acceptance towards those who are culturally divergent?

The stories of Corrie ten Boom and the servant girl of Naaman inform us that it is indeed possible. The teachings of Jesus lead us to the same conclusion.

You have heard that it was said, "Love your neighbor and hate your enemy." But I tell you, love your enemies and pray for those who persecute you, that you may be children of your Father in heaven. He causes his sun to rise on the evil and the good, and sends rain on the righteous and the unrighteous. If you love those who love you, what reward will you get? Are not even the tax collectors doing that? And if you greet only your own people, what are you doing more than others? Do not even pagans do that? Be perfect, therefore, as your heavenly Father is perfect.
- Matthew 5:43-48

> *Have you witnessed people who seem to easily love the foreigner, even when they are traditional enemies? How do you think that happens?*

Jesus teaches us that by loving our enemies we are enabled to be children of our Father in heaven. That's pretty tough language to be able to meld with a deep-seated emotional nationalism that leads to atrocities against humanity. In fact, many would be happy to just dismiss that statement of Jesus. "He really can't expect us to love our enemies, can He?" On the contrary, he not only expects it, he commands it, and he enables us. He is the one who enables us to love, because it is his nature.

> *What are some practical first steps you could take to help restore a relationship marked by distrust, hatred and fear? Are there ways these steps could be leveraged on a broader scale to reach the immigrants living among us?*

Consider these words from the Apostle Paul to the Christians at Rome:

You see, at just the right time, when we were still powerless, Christ died for the ungodly. Very rarely will anyone die for a righteous person, though for a good person someone might possibly dare to die. But God demonstrates his own love for us in this: While we were still sinners, Christ died for us.

Since we have now been justified by his blood, how much more shall we be saved from God's wrath through him! For if, while we were God's enemies, we were reconciled to him through the death of his Son, how much more, having been reconciled, shall we be saved through his life!
–Romans 5:6-10

> *Read Romans 5:1-5. How does Paul describe the process of being filled with God's love? Are you comfortable with that process? What might you need to do to submit your will to God's will in this matter?*

Don't miss how Paul identifies the readers and when God acted on their behalf,

"When we were still powerless…Christ died for the ungodly"
"While we were still sinners…Christ died for us"
"While we were God's enemies…we were reconciled to him"

> *In what specific ways has your sense of nationalism trumped your compassion for an individual or group of people?*

If God acted in Christ when we were powerless, while we were his enemies, and when we were God's enemies, we can know that his power is enough to enable us to love those for whom we have held long-term hatred or apathy. It is not simply a matter of the strength of our will. It is the power of Christ at work within us.

> *Is there one person for whom it is difficult for you to extend the hand of forgiveness? Name that person and ask your group to pray with you that God would give you His forgiveness for this person.*

Questions for Further Reflection:

1. What trends can you see over time that perpetuate hatred for a certain nationality?

2. Who are the people you find most difficult to love? Why?

3. Identify any current cultural trends that might run contrary to the command to love our enemy.

4. What do you think God might do in your life to break down any long-seated hatred toward another people group?

5. What could you or your small group do to create an atmosphere of love and acceptance towards those who are culturally divergent?

6. Have you witnessed people who seem to easily love the foreigner, even when they are traditional enemies? How do you think that happens?

7. What are some practical first steps you could take to help restore a relationship marked by distrust, hatred and fear? Are there ways these steps could be leveraged on a broader scale to reach the immigrants living among us?

8. Read Romans 5:1-5. How does Paul describe the process of being filled with God's love? Are you comfortable with that process? What might you need to do to submit your will to God's will in this matter?

9. In what specific ways has your sense of nationalism trumped your compassion for an individual or group of people?

10. Is there one person for whom it is difficult for you to extend the hand of forgiveness? Name that person and ask your group to pray with you that God would give you His forgiveness for this person.

INCREASE INTERNALLY: GOING BEYOND THE EXPECTED

In 2003 our church began to pray for the Lord to send us into the neighborhood. At that time, we had relatively few, if any, people other than the majority ethnicity of our city. We were white on white. This is nothing against the church—most churches find themselves homogenous. But when we began praying, I think our expectation was that God would send us into our mostly white neighborhoods.

As we continued to pray, we had a visit from a woman of Chinese descent who was married to a man from Puerto Rico. We loved them. They stuck. Our pastor fell in love with this couple and began to learn the needs of the many Chinese in our community. Before long we put a simple sign out in the church yard that was in Chinese. It said, "Learn to speak English here." At the same time our pastor and his wife began visiting Chinese restaurants. They developed a network of friendships, and soon we were having late night restaurant fellowships. These usually started about 11 p.m. and lasted until 1 or 2 a.m.

In a few years our church hired a missionary from Taiwan to come and be the spiritual leader for our Chinese-speaking families. In time we planted a new congregation which has grown consistently in its scope and mission. Since then a house church has been planted for those from China who are visiting the United States. In the past 15 years there have been scores of conversions and baptisms. Many have returned to China to share the gospel.

Recently, this same church has had an influx of people from the Democratic Republic of the Congo and Tanzania. They are being enfolded into the life of the church, and all the while, those of us who are white are becoming more like Jesus with them.

It has been exciting and hard. There have been ups and downs along the way, but the key is, the church had no expectation of what God was going to do. They were just willing.

> **What are some changes that have happened in the church that have made you uncomfortable? Are the changes threatening to doctrine or just functional changes? What are the most common reasons people resist change?**

It reminds me of what transpired in the early church. The early church was centered in Jerusalem with good people of Jewish descent. In fact, on the day of Pentecost, those who were saved were either Jews or converts to Judaism. It wasn't until the martyrdom of Stephen that the church really even ventured out beyond Jerusalem. But with his death a great persecution broke out.

> On that day a great persecution broke out against the church in Jerusalem, and all except the apostles were scattered throughout Judea and Samaria … Those who had been scattered preached the word wherever they went.
> – Acts 8:1,4

> **Where is Jerusalem, Judea, and Samaria for you? For your church?**

Philip, the deacon, preached in Samaria. Peter and John followed up and preached in many Samaritan villages. I have wondered, if the persecution had not happened, would the disciples have ever made it out of Jerusalem? It certainly does not seem to have happened by strategic planning.

Peter ends up traveling throughout the country preaching at Lydda and Sharon and also in Joppa, where he stays with Simon the Tanner. While he is there, the Lord is working on a man named Cornelius. He lives in Caesarea. He is a God-fearing Gentile. He has a vision where he sees an angel of God who tells him to send a messenger to Joppa to bring back a man named Simon who is called Peter. So Cornelius sends two servants to fetch Simon Peter.

Meanwhile, Peter has a dream about unclean animals, which repeats three times. The conclusion from Peter is that he should not call anything unclean that God has called clean. About this time the men from Cornelius arrive. Paul invites them in to be his overnight guests.

The next day they set out for Caesarea and arrive the following day. Even though Peter is hesitant himself to go into the house of a Gentile, he understood the dream and enters.

> **For Peter to go to Cornelius, it took a special dream and vision from the Lord. How does that confront or comfort you?**

Peter listens to Cornelius' account of his encounter with the angel. Peter said, "I now realize how true it is that God does not show favoritism but accepts from every nation the one who fears him and does what is right." Before Peter finishes his message the Holy Spirit comes on all the Gentile believers just like he had come on the day of Pentecost.

> **Peter was able to make a transference from the vision about the unclean animals to understanding that he shouldn't call any person unclean because of their ethnicity. What ways, if any, do you hold a view about a certain people group that needs to be altered? How is God speaking to you about this?**

There is no one in all Judaism or Christianity at that point who would have predicted that outcome. There was no strategic plan to reach the Gentiles. It was simply God opening the doors and thrusting the apostles through it.

It took the church a little while to figure it out, but the key was the dependency on the Holy Spirit to lead. It was the spontaneous expansion of the church from Judaism to the rest of humanity.

> **As you reflect on the movement of the early church from being only Jewish to crossing the walls to reach the rest of the nations, what would you consider to be the biggest obstacles facing the expansion of the church in America today?**

I have seen spontaneous expansion happen more than once. It is exciting and unnerving. I have seen it happen more in crossing cultural barriers than I have in homogenous ministry. I'm not contending that it doesn't happen there; it is just my experience to see it happen more frequently when God is opening new doors.

Here is the challenge for cross-cultural ministry: we have to be open to the spontaneity of the Holy Spirit. It might take us to neighborhoods we wouldn't otherwise choose to enter. It might bring people to us we aren't familiar with. We might even be called to eat food we have never eaten before.

> **How do you generally respond to a spontaneous change of plans? Why do you think some people are quicker to embrace change than others?**

Several years ago we began to pray this prayer from Jim Cymbala, "Bring us the drug-addicted, bring us the prostitutes, bring us the destitute, bring us the gang leaders, bring us those with AIDS, bring us the people nobody else wants, whom only you can heal, and let us love them in your name until they are whole." God began to answer our prayer. He began to send up people nobody else wanted. It was hard. There are reasons nobody else wanted them. But we loved.

Most of those people were not like us. But that was okay, because we are not much like God and he accepted us and gave his only Son to die for us. So we adjusted. If the Holy Spirit leads, adjust.

That's the beauty of the gospel. We can adjust methods. We can adjust time. We can adjust style. Because the one constant is not cultural; it is eternal. It is Jesus.

> Jesus Christ is the same yesterday and today and forever.
> - Hebrews 13:8

Is there any place you are unwilling to go to share about Jesus? What is it that keeps you from going?

One of the key concepts at the birth of the Free Methodist Church was spontaneity. I used to think it was because of how starchy the Methodist Episcopal Church had become. But I have since altered my view. I think it is more in line with the original mission of the church, "To maintain the Bible standard of Christianity, and to preach the Gospel to the poor." If you are going to reach the poor, you have to be spontaneous. Spontaneity assumes flexibility.

When God calls you to reach across cultural barriers, he at the same time calls you to be flexible and to love change.

What are the differences between doctrinal change and functional change? Why is it important to make a distinction?

Questions for Further Reflection:

1. What are some changes that have happened in the church that have made you uncomfortable? Are the changes threatening to doctrine or just functional changes?

2. What are the most common reasons people resist change?

3. Where is Jerusalem, Judea, and Samaria for you? For your church?

4. For Peter to go to Cornelius, it took a special dream and vision from the Lord. How does that confront or comfort you?

5. Peter was able to make a transference from the vision about the unclean animals to understanding that he shouldn't call any person unclean because of their ethnicity. What ways, if any, do you hold a view about a certain people group that needs to be altered? How is God speaking to you about this?

6. As you reflect on the movement of the early church from being only Jewish to crossing the walls to reach the rest of the nations, what would you consider to be the biggest obstacles facing the expansion of the church in America today?

7. How do you generally respond to a spontaneous change of plans?

8. Why do you think some people are quicker to embrace change than others?

9. Is there any place you are unwilling to go to share about Jesus? What is it that keeps you from going?

10. What are the differences between doctrinal change and functional change? Why is it important to make a distinction?

BROADEN BIBLICALLY:
UNDERSTANDING HOSPITALITY

There is this story in the book of Acts that exemplifies the way we need to enter into the target culture's community in order to be trusted. It is a simple line found in Acts 16.

> **When someone asks you to be hospitable, what do you assume that means?**

On the Sabbath we went outside the city gate to the river, where we expected to find a place of prayer. We sat down and began to speak to the women who had gathered there. One of those listening was a woman from the city of Thyatira named Lydia, a dealer in purple cloth. She was a worshiper of God. The Lord opened her heart to respond to Paul's message. When she and the members of her household were baptized, she invited us to her home. "If you consider me a believer in the Lord," she said, "come and stay at my house." And she persuaded us.
–Acts 16:13-15

> **What can you learn from your experience as an outsider that helps you to love others?**

Lydia was a merchant and most likely Greek. She responded to the message from Paul. But she immediately wants to know if she is accepted or not. "If you consider me a believer in the Lord, come and stay at my house." Lydia is offering her acceptance of Paul and his companions. It would have been a cultural insult to refuse, even though it might not have had anything to do with whether or not Paul thought Lydia to be a believer. Paul and his companions had already been in Philippi several days. They had arrangements for housing. So this invitation is more than just providing a place; it is an invitation of acceptance. It is simple: "If you consider me a believer in the Lord…"

> **What are some situations where you felt like you were the outsider? How did someone welcome you, or fail to welcome you?**

The Gentile world knew the ways of the Jews well. They knew that Jews were not supposed to enter into their houses. Paul, a Jew by birth, is now put to the test by a simple invitation. Lydia's question might be put in another way: "Is the gospel really open to me? Will it break down these barriers?"

> **How is being kind or welcoming to a stranger or foreigner part of loving them?**

Paul would later write to the Ephesians,

> For he himself is our peace, who has made the two groups one and has destroyed the barrier, the dividing wall of hostility, by setting aside in his flesh the law with its commands and regulations. His purpose was to create in himself one new humanity out of the two, thus making peace, and in one body to reconcile both of them to God through the cross, by which he put to death their hostility.
> - Ephesians 2:14-16

Lydia wanted to know if she was a friend. Was she fully accepted or just conditionally accepted? I wonder if that encounter helped Paul develop his theology. For he would continue in his writing to the Ephesians, "Consequently, you are no longer foreigners and strangers, but fellow citizens with God's people and also members of his household, built on the foundation of the apostles and prophets, with Christ Jesus himself as the chief cornerstone." (Ephesians 2:19-20)

> **How would loving a foreigner be extended beyond just being kind or welcoming?**

The big question that was constantly before the early church was the full inclusion of the Gentiles solely on faith in Jesus Christ. It is the same question from Lydia — "Am I really considered by you to be a believer?" It is still the question many have on their minds. Can I become a Christian and keep my ethnic identity? Or is your Christianity simply an expression of Western culture?

> **What kinds of things can you do to build friendships with people who are immigrants to our country?**

The key is found in hospitality. When I use that word many people will immediately think of someone who is able to host a wonderful party, or able to welcome guest into their home. And those are good things. But the biblical base for hospitality is found in the word itself—*philoxenia*. The word literally means "love of strangers" or "love of foreigners."

One of the ways to practice love of strangers is to adapt to their ways, to visit in their homes, to eat their food. On my first trip to the Philippines our missionary told me, "Gerry, there are two ways into the culture; speak their language or eat their food. You won't be here long enough to learn the language, so eat the food." I have done so with great joy in every culture I have visited!

> **What are other passages in the Bible that instruct us on how to care for foreigners?**

I have watched several churches successfully bridge the gap to another ethnic group in their city. They seem to do a few things really well. They teach English. They help with practical skills like getting a driver's license and learning how to shop our stores. They eat the food. These are visible expressions of love of foreigners.

Another thing these churches do successfully is accept the foreigners' ways. The churches are intentional about not promoting American culture as superior. Cultural practices aren't usually a matter of better or worse, just different.

In our connection with Chinese people living in America, we have different views toward medicine. Our Chinese friends have given us herbal remedies and even massage techniques to deal with medical issues for which we would take a pill. We accept their gifts. We have found they are at least as effective, if not more, than our ways. In the meantime we have built a bridge by valuing their way.

> **What are the tensions in our own society that foster xenophobia *rather than* philoxenia?**

Another visible expression of love of foreigners is the giving of gifts appropriate to their cultural traditions. We had to search the internet for when certain groups give gifts and what an appropriate gift would be. To be honest, we made some mistakes. But it didn't seem to matter too much. People knew we were trying to express love.

And the heart of hospitality is true love. Over ten years ago, the Lord put in my heart a love for people that transcended my previous understanding. I came to understand that the Lord loves unconditionally whether or not a person ever comes to faith in Christ. That put aside all my pretenses to love in order to win people to Christ. I was laid bare to the core, realizing that previously I had loved people for a purpose. Now I was being called to love them no matter what. What I found was liberty to love. Performance and expectations were set aside. I became a lover of people simply because God loves people.

How has the Biblical definition of the word hospitality broadened your understanding?

There is no substitute for biblical hospitality, and there is no other source than Jesus Christ. It was his instruction to his disciples, "A new command I give you: Love one another. As I have loved you, so you must love one another. By this everyone will know that you are my disciples, if you love one another." -John 13:34-35

"Practice hospitality" was Paul's instruction to the church at Rome, a church that was struggling because it was made up of Jews and Gentiles. The word was straightforward—"Love the strangers!" "Love the foreigners!" Paul had lived it out in his own life, and now through the enduring word we know as the Bible, he calls us all to this same love.

Commit with another person to take specific action to welcome a foreigner this week. Then set an appointment when you will check up on each other to see how things went.

Questions for Further Reflection:

1. When someone asks you to be hospitable, what do you assume that means?

2. How has the Biblical definition of the word hospitality broadened your understanding?

3. What are other passages in the Bible that instruct us on how to care for foreigners?

4. What are the tensions in our own society that foster xenophobia rather than philoxenia?

5. What are some situations where you felt like you were the outsider? How did someone welcome you, or fail to welcome you?

6. What can you learn from your experience as an outsider that helps you to love others?

7. How is being kind or welcoming to a stranger or foreigner part of loving them?

8. How would loving a foreigner be extended beyond just being kind or welcoming?

9. What kinds of things can you do to build friendships with people who are immigrants to our country?

10. Commit with another person to take specific action to welcome a foreigner this week. Then set an appointment when you will check up on each other to see how things went.

CONCLUSION

The Free Methodist Church is expanding rapidly in many parts of the world. The Church is partnering with the Holy Spirit planting churches and developing leaders. Not only are nearly 95% of Free Methodists located outside the United States, most Free Methodists do not worship in a church building. For those of us in the United States, we are coming to realize the worldwide Free Methodist Church has much to teach us about following Jesus.

Now is not the time to disengage, but to participate more fully in global ministry. Not only can we provide much-needed financial and educational resources, we have much to gain as learners from the international church. Every opportunity to engage with another culture is an opportunity to learn more about Jesus and his kingdom.

From the beginning of the church, the vision has been for a multicultural church. The instruction of Jesus was to go the Jerusalem, Judea, Samaria and to the ends of the earth. The vision John was given was of believers gathered around the throne of the Lamb from every language, tribe, people, and nation. In our day-to-day life in the United States, it is easy to think the kingdom centers on us, but Scripture and history tell a much broader story and paint a more beautiful picture of the kingdom.

We are called not only to recognize the inherent sinfulness of current trends toward ethnocentrism and xenophobia, but to champion the cause of the kingdom of God, here on earth as it is in heaven. Whether it is by going as a pioneering missionary or investing to help send them, or partnering with the international church, or building relationships in your own city with people of other cultural origins, you are called to Go Global.

FINAL THOUGHT

Knowing God is the highest priority of humanity, because knowing God changes us. We hope that this issue has given you a fresh perspective and equipped you with the raw materials God can use to keep you learning the Way of Jesus.

Sincerely,
Dr. David McDonald
Editor, FreeMo Journals

DISCIPLE DEEPLY
BY DR. DAVID MCDONALD WITH MARK VAN VALIN

The original twelve disciples were thickheaded, ego-driven, and blind; so, clearly, you don't have to be perfect in order to follow Jesus. But it seems like we give ourselves too much leeway to behave poorly, to think sloppily, or to interact disingenuously. Because "nobody's perfect" we don't put a lot of effort into the process of our ongoing perfection.

We ought to change that.

EMBRACE ALL
BY JOANNA DEWOLF

The best stories only get better over time and nothing captures our hearts like the story of Jesus' birth.

HONORING FRUITFULNESS
BY RICK CALLAHAN

Jesus offers an abundant life–a life that is deep and wide, full of meaning and purpose.

CULTIVATING HEALTH
BY CHERYL WAYMAN

Why is it so hard to heal our broken relationships? How can God transform not only our relationships but our emotions
as well?

PARTNER STRONG
BY BEN REDMOND

Partnership is not an optional endeavor for those of us who follow Jesus. God has placed us in this exact moment of human history, and He has chosen us as His partners. Not based on our resume or talent. No, God picks His partners based on availability over ability.

So now it's our turn to partner with God, with each other, and with the world as we find our place in the greatest story of them all.

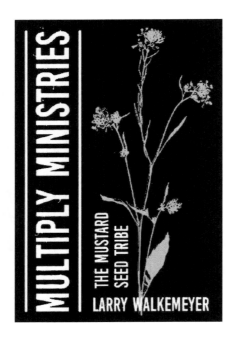

MULTIPLY MINISTRIES
BY LARRY WALKEMEYER

Mustard plants are one of the most remarkable plants in God's garden. As a spice, mustard is only surpassed in importance by salt and pepper. It is one of the hardiest and most generative herbs. Mustard multiplies.

As followers of Jesus we are often tempted to look in the mirror at our own limited dimensions and envision the future based on the reflection we see. What can I do? How much can my ministry accomplish? How can our little church have an impact?
How can we leave a significant legacy?

The answer?

Multiply.

THE EYES OF THE NATIVITY
BY JOHN VOELZ

There are stories we casually enjoy and then there are stories that compel us to act. This book has 13 chapters about the nativity. Each one looks at the nativity through different eyes—different stages of life, different responsibilities and roles.

It's easy to fall in the trap of telling the Christmas narrative with the enthusiasm of someone reciting Hickory Dickory Dock. But, if we pay attention, the nativity will propel us to follow Christ confidently not as though he were far away, but because we know him as Immanuel: God with us.

SHADOWING GOD
BY DAVID MCDONALD

God wants to do more in us
and through us than for us and to us.

God's ways are subtle, and they are all around us, but we don't often perceive him or his work in the world because we are looking for something clumsy and big to show us our destiny.

We must learn to see God's activity in the world just behind the one we see, in the shadows, toward the wings, and just off-stage.

But once we pay attention to what's happening just behind everything we see with our eyes, we are introduced to another world, to a better world, and a better life in it.

DEVELOPING LEADERS
BY DR. ROB MCKENNA

Incarnational leaders and disciples have something in common - a desire to follow Jesus.

The path to growth has less to do with ascension and upward movement. The path to growth always starts with a sacrifice.

This book is designed to cultivate your character, an essential component of both Christian discipleship and leadership. You can use this material to make disciples in your church, at work, and in your family. How is this possible? Again, both leadership and discipleship are dependent upon faithfully following Jesus, so the emphasis of this book is on the formation of Christ-like character.

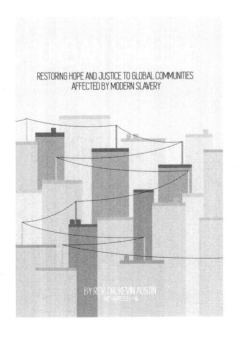

RESTORING HOPE AND JUSTICE TO GLOBAL COMMUNITIES AFFECTED BY MODERN SLAVERY

URBAN SHALOM
BY REV. DR. KEVIN AUSTIN WITH KATIE BERGMAN

As Christians, our own liberation compels us to help liberate others, seeking justice for those who are enslaved spiritually, emotionally, or even physically by modern-day slave holders known as human traffickers. Our goal is transformation: starting with the character of God, moving into compassionate communities, being rooted in Jesus, and then engaging in God's mission of shalom where harmful values are shifted and relationships are restored.

The FreeMo Journal is published quarterly (Fall, Christmas, January, Easter, and Summer). Subscriptions are available through Light + Life Communication and previous issues can be ordered from The Wesleyan Publishing House at (800) 493.7539.

IF YOU'RE INTERESTED IN WRITING FOR THE FREEMO JOURNAL, PLEASE CONTACT DAVID.MCDONALD@FMCUSA.ORG